EveryMom

How I Survived
a Toddler and a Newborn on a
Promise and a Prayer

Megan Lagoy

To my Lord, who walks with me through all of my days.

To my husband, who believes in me, always.

To Aunt Teri, Bethany, Mom, Celeste, and Lindsay, who spurred me on to write better, do better, and be better. "Without counsel, plans go awry, but in the multitude of counselors they are established" (Proverbs 15:22).

An extra thanks to Lindsay, who read every word I wrote and revised and rewrote...all the while being an inspiring mother to three beautiful girls.

To the uber-grandparents in my life: Mimi and Boppa, who never hesitate to make time when we need them; and Lolo and Lola, who, although they are farther away, can't wait to hug on their grandkids and <u>never</u> come empty handed.

To Isaac, who keeps me on my toes.

And especially to Abby, whose innocent arrival into the world sparked a new journey for me as a mother and as a woman.

Cover design by Darrell Picha

Photos by Adel Lagoy

The traditional ending to all Lagoy brother-sister photo shoots...

...it's either that, or tears.

Here are my other subtitle ideas for this book. Most of them were rejected for obvious reasons:

EveryMom: The Diary of a Mad Woman (Who Happens to Have Two Young Children)

EveryMom: Two Kids; Terrible Twos; Too Much for This Momma

EveryMom: My Kids Are Twenty-One Months Apart, God Help Me

EveryMom: One Toddler + One Newborn = More Than My Hand's Full

EveryMom: Help Me God! I Have Two Kids Under Two!

EveryMom: I'm in Over My Head Now

EveryMom: What, oh *What* Have I Gotten Myself Into?

EveryMom: We're All in This Together, Momma (So Pass the Chocolate)

EveryMom: Help! My Small Children are Eating Me Alive!

EveryMom: Raising Two Kids Under Two and Going Insane

EveryMom: Did I Mention I'm Raising Two Kids Under Two?

EveryMom: Raising Two Kids and... Isaac, Let Go of Abby's Hair!!!

EveryMom: Due to "Mommy's Brain" Syndrome, I Can't Remember
What I Was Going to Say Here, But I'm Sure It Was Really Important

Contents

Introduction

Let me set the scene for this book:

Having just moved to Texas, I'm adjusting to a new climate and a new culture. (Yeehaw) Initially, I'm without community and friendless in my new home. (Anyone up for a cup of coffee...anyone...*anyone!?*) Isaac, my first born, is twenty-one months old and wild as a game hen. (I said, put that down, son!) And the rules of motherhood seem to keep changing on me. (Wait, now you hate napping?) I'm the old-school kind of stay-at-home mom: no housekeeper, no mother's-day-out program, no super nanny, no personal chef. (Just me. All day long. With my feisty child.) And if that's not enough to make any mom lose her mind, I'm also naïve and optimistic, easily crushed when things don't go the way I had imagined. (And I whine a lot.)

Then I give birth to my second child. I thought I had it rough before, but after Abby's birth I learn that chaos has a whole new meaning. It's not that Abby by herself is any trouble. It's just that, with two children, I'm having to learn it's quite impossible to have everyone content all the time. At times, somebody has to cry. And sometimes it's me!

And what do I have going for me? Actually, quite a lot. I have: a husband who is loving and reliable; an extended family that's closer in proximity than ever before and willing to help in my crisis moments; a new friendship that helps me start to feel at home in this new place; a desire to write down (vent) my experiences, a Book of God's promises (the Bible!); and my daily cries for help to a God who not only listens, but also cares.

In spite of the title, this book is not a foreshadowing of what *every mom* should expect to experience. How could I ever claim to know what another mom's motherhood experience will be like? Our situations are as diverse as our God-given uniqueness. However, I do hope that there are many stories here that my readers can relate to. I think that *every mom*, regardless of her unique experience, has a common thread woven into the sisterhood of mothers. We are individuals, but there is something about this job that unifies us. I pray that as you chuckle at my foibles as a mother, you will relate to my struggles and develop with me a passionate, enduring reliance on God.

And finally, this book is not for moms who have it all together. If God did not see fit to endow me with abundant wisdom and with-it-ness (let me just say it, He didn't), He at least seems to have granted me transparency. This book is my honest experience with this stage of motherhood and the messes I get myself into. So, those blissful "with-it" mommas who get it right, all the time, would read this book with scorn. That type of mom would just think I'm a basket case who's flubbing this whole motherhood thing. And she'd be right of course, but I don't need her to tell me that! No, this book is not for *that* type of mom.

This is a book for moms who:

- wonder, on a daily basis, what they are doing wrong
- love their children beyond description, yet can't wait to get away from them

- feel like they're an inch away from throwing the biggest temper tantrum their toddlers have ever seen
- love being stay-at-home moms, yet believe naptime is the best time of day
- cry sometimes because being a mom can be so hard
- feel guilty for having to remind themselves that children are a blessing
- love mommy's night out almost as much as their first-born child
- wonder if they can find motherhood to be this challenging and still be good mothers

Sometimes, we mothers just need to be real with each other so that we know we're not alone. I'll go first. This book is the chronicle of a real mother who wants to let other real mothers know that being real is okay. (And God obviously has a sense of humor. If He didn't, He wouldn't have created boogers, poop, or toddlers in general.) In short, this is not a book about being a perfect mom. Rather, this is a book about being an *im*perfect mom, wrapped in the arms of God's perfect grace.

Family Planning

I have always assumed my kids would be born about two years apart. My sister and I are just over two years apart and it seemed to work out fine. We *almost* never tried to kill each other. That's pretty good, right? (We're really close now, going through the same phases of motherhood together.)

I never really gave my own family planning strategy too much thought. Popping out a kid every two years or so just seemed like the way it was done. In retrospect, I am learning that generally, and *especially* when it comes to childrearing, this method of thoughtless action is not the wisest option.

Nonetheless, when Isaac turned thirteen months old, Adel and I stopped using birth control. The next time we sat down in the same room together, we instantly became pregnant. We actually thought it would take several months to get pregnant, but apparently God couldn't wait to teach us the lesson of a lifetime.

At first we were excited. Then, as my belly began to swell and Isaac began to morph from a baby to a toddler, we began to guess at what lay in store for us. Abby's due date neared while Isaac continued to grow in speed, aerodynamics, agility, destructive capacity, and

13

general tenacity. Adel and I began to say out loud the thought that had been creeping up on us individually for months: "What, *oh what* have we done to ourselves?"

We were learning that in life with a toddler, every task becomes a dance of one step forward, two steps back. As I folded the clean t-shirts, Isaac would be unrolling the clean socks. As I hung the new baby clothes, he would be pulling all the shoes off the rack. As I brushed my teeth, he would pull all the soap packages out from under my sink and unwrap them. I might get one thing accomplished but somehow in the same amount of time, he would add two more tasks to my list.

And I know this is not an unusual experience for mothers of toddlers. The examples of toddler mayhem are endless. In fact, I've generated a catalog below with dozens of possibilities. You can pretty much match up any action from the column on the left to any object from the column on the right and I'm sure that we can find a toddler somewhere who has accomplished that feat. You know you're the parent of a toddler if you find your child...

ACTION	OBJECT
Dumping	the trashcan
Tasting	the dog food
Hitting	the cat
Throwing	the spoon
Climbing	the bookcase
Running around	the table
Standing on	the book
Biting	the sibling
Pulling	the toilet paper
Writing on	the refrigerator
Jumping on	the couch
Kicking	the dog
Licking	the shoes

14

So you may have a toddler who has tasted the dog food *or the dog*. Your toddler may have thrown the book *or the cat*. If you're not paying attention it's even possible that your child may right now be writing on the refrigerator *or the even the sibling*. You should probably be paying more attention to that child before he gets into serious trouble.

Speaking of that, Isaac...what are you up to now? Licking the table? Not posing imminent danger to yourself or others? Good boy.

It was into this toddler-crazed home that I was knowingly going to add a precious newborn! Let us repeat with fear and trembling: "What, *oh what* have we done to ourselves?"

A PROMISE

"Fear not, for I have redeemed you; I have called you by your name; you are Mine. When you pass through the waters, I will be with you; and through the rivers, they shall not overflow you. When you walk through the fire, you shall not be burned, nor shall the flame scorch you" (Isaiah 43:1b-2).

A PRAYER

Lord, I admit I am anxious (and a little fearful) about what is to come. You never promised that life would be easy all the time, but You did promise to be with me when things get tough! Please give me Your grace, Your wisdom, and Your strength as new challenges come forth. It gives me great comfort to know that I do not have to do this alone and I eagerly await the precious gift of life You plan to give me.

Second Birth

A PERSPECTIVE

Everything was different the second time around. Since Isaac's nine-pound-four-ounce bulk had been so difficult to deliver, I decided to get induced a few days before Abby's due date. (Why not? Everybody's doing it these days. And yes, Mom, if they all jumped off a cliff, I probably would too.) This time I walked into the hospital early in the morning with no signs of impending labor. It is strange to be in such a clear frame of mind and understand that when you walk out again the baby will be on the *outside* of your body!

This was so different from my first experience. When I was wheeled into the hospital with Isaac I was incoherently moaning:

Nurse: Ma'am, before we admit you to the hospital to deliver your baby, I need you to sign here and here, and initial here.

Me: Argggggghhhhhhhh!!!

Actually, what I was thinking was, "I'm writhing in pain every thirty seconds. I'm unable to walk upright, keep my eyes from rolling back in their sockets, or release my death grip on the armrest of this

16

wheelchair, and you want me to do *what*?!?!" But all I managed to say was "Arggggggghhhhhhhh" while I smeared some unintelligible ink marks on whatever piece of paper she shoved under my nose. I might have signed away my vast fortune and never would have been the wiser. It's a good thing I don't have a vast fortune.

So, right from the start, we were already doing better with Abby's delivery. I chatted pleasantly with my nurse as she hooked me up, using various tubes and needles, to "the machine" to start my contractions. Then Adel and I watched *The Cosby Show* for a couple hours while my belly gently contracted. Eventually my doctor came in, broke my bag of waters, and made a few swift adjustments to the amount of contraction-inducing substance that "the machine" was pumping into my body via the various tubes and needles. That's when labor really kicked in.

Up to this point I had been managing quite nicely without pain medication. With both births, I had the philosophy that I would get an epidural when and *if* (ha!) I needed it, and not a moment before. I wanted to "experience" the births of my children as much as possible. Well, as soon as the doctor broke my water and those contractions made me feel that I was being punctured by a million Lilliputian swords, I decided that I had just about enough of this birth "experience." I asked for my epidural: "Drugs…now…please!"

My mom and sister arrived as the epidural was taking effect. We chatted between contractions for about half an hour and then Abby started crowning. Really, it was that fast. So fast, in fact, that I thought I just had to go to the bathroom really bad. And the pain came back immediately as Abby made her descent. It was suddenly as if I had no epidural at all. It felt like a pumpkin being carved and hollowed for Halloween. The pain was familiar: *Oh yeah, I remember this. This is why I swore I would never give birth again after having Isaac. Who tricked me into doing this again? What? It was my own idea? Don't I know better by now than to listen to a word I say?*

17

Then came the delivery. My previous experience with birthing a child is that you have to push for hours with no functioning epidural and then finally beg the doctor to use whatever bizarre tool she has available to just get the child out of there. That's how it was with Isaac. That little man was happy with the status quo and put up a huge fight. Come to think of it, it's strangely ironic: stubborn in birth, stubborn in life!

With Abby, it took the doctor a few minutes to arrive and by the time she was set up, I was already pushing. Abby came flying out a few pushes later. Her flight was a bit alarming as no one expected it to be so sudden. (Especially me. I was thinking, "Okay that was push number four out of eight hundred and fifty-two. Pace yourself, momma!"). In actuality, the doctor had just said, "Her head is out," and turned around to grab something from the table of instruments behind her. With the doctor's back turned, Abby flew out like a greased watermelon down a slip n' slide. If the doctor hadn't caught her, Abby would have slid right off the table.

The whole delivery was over before lunchtime, just a few hours after it began. Pretty different from the first time around with the eighteen-hour-labor experience. I must say this second birth was much more pleasant. And the strange irony of Abby's debut into the world: easy-going in birth, easy-going in life.

Before Abby's birth, I had been wondering, like every other second-time mom, is it possible to love another child even half as much as you love your first? After Abby made her slippery and speedy debut into my arms, the answer was completely, irrevocably, and without hesitation, *yes!* I would say, for those first two days at the hospital, I was pretty wrapped up in love for my new baby girl. There, with Abby's angelic hands folded under her cupid cheek as she slept on my lap, my essential question had changed. It was no longer, *will I love her as much as I love Isaac?* It was more like, *Isaac who?*

Then somewhere in the transition home, I began to miss my boy. I was thrilled to see him again when we returned home. And the separate love I feel for each of my children is somehow both paramount *and* tantamount, both unsurpassed *and* equal. I love Isaac more than anyone in the world. *And* I love Abby more than anyone in the world. I don't know how I do this. I just do.

A PROMISE

"A woman, when she is in labor, has sorrow because her hour has come; but as soon as she has given birth to the child, she no longer remembers the anguish, for joy that a human being has been born into the world" (John 16:21).

A PRAYER

I praise You, Lord, for the joy of bringing two new human beings into the world in just two short years. Thank You for filling new mothers and repeat mothers alike with overflowing love for their new children, like the abundance of the Holy Spirit being poured into our hearts.

Not a Baby Anymore

A PERSPECTIVE

The night before I went in to the hospital to be induced with Abby, I remember saying goodnight to my twenty-one-month-old baby, Isaac. It was very emotional. For one thing, I knew I was going to miss him for the two days of hospital stay. (I had already decided that he should not come to visit us. He was so clingy that bringing him in for a short visit and then taking him away again would be like ripping a bandage off a fresh wound. Ouch.) But more than just missing him for a few days, I also knew that some major changes were going to take place in my relationship with him. The next time I saw him, Isaac would no longer be my baby.

When we came home, he ran to greet us with a huge smile. Then he stared suspiciously at the strange infant in the car seat. We had been telling him the baby in Mommy's tummy was his little sister Abby. So he knew right away that the baby was his Abby:

Us: (*pointing to the baby*) Isaac, who's this?

Isaac: Abby-Sister!

20

Once we had settled in, I noticed a change in my perspective right away. The first thing I observed was that Isaac was HUGE. I had been gone for two days, changing little newborn diapers. The first time after our return that I changed Isaac's size four, I was shocked at how big his tushie was. It was like caring for a newborn pixy and then suddenly being asked to change the diaper of Colossus of Rhodes. That's a lot of tushie. Truly, he was not a baby anymore!

Our relationship changed too. Ah, the good old days of being an only child! They were great while they lasted, weren't they little buddy? But now they're gone. Now, there's a new little person with entirely different needs. Let's just say Isaac did not enjoy the transition from being a momma's boy to being the *other* child. It's not like he went from being king of the world to chopped liver over night. It actually took *three* nights. Okay, really he never became chopped liver at all (or even close). He just had to adjust to the universe having two centers.

I think this transition may not be as difficult for other kids, but Isaac has always been glued to my side (not necessarily by my choice). For example, it took over two weeks of living with Mimi and Boppa (my parents) during our move to Texas before he would let his grandparents hold him without crying for Momma. He apparently mistook them for the Grinch and Mr. Scrooge before realizing that they are actually kind of nice (and one of them is a female).

Having a little sister vying for Momma's attention really made matters worse. If I happened to be so audacious as to be carrying Abby in my arms when picking Isaac up from his nap, he would instantly freak out: "No Abby. No Abby!!!" And later, "Put Abby down, Mom!" He even became jealous of Abby's diaper changes, throwing himself on the ground and crying for me to hold him or change *his* diaper. I would have to tell him, "I already changed your diaper, Colossus." Of course I tried to do whatever I could to give him the attention he craved and I always let him know how much I love him. But there was just no way to curb his insatiable appetite for mommy-dominion.

Obviously, this transition forced Isaac to quickly become more independent in certain areas. He accepted his independence *very* reluctantly. He had to go up and down stairs by himself since I was usually holding Abby (although I confess to carrying both children up and down quite regularly to appease the boy's whims). He had to learn to climb into his car seat so that I could put Abby in hers (he actually enjoyed this one). He also had to learn to keep himself occupied while I nursed and tended to Abby. His preferred activities to keep himself occupied were:

- Utter destruction of a household object
- Full-throttled wailing for attention at his mother's feet
- Hyper-active bursts of energy, usually involving clambering up his mother's legs and bouncing on her stomach or head, regardless of the fact that she was holding a nursing newborn
-

Thus, in my mind's eye, Isaac morphed from being the baby to being the exasperating older brother who kept waking up the baby. Our car rides are the perfect illustration. Infant Abby, like her older brother before her, passionately hated her car seat. If she was awake in it, she was crying. So, at the end of the long drive to Mimi and Boppa's house, I would exit the freeway as smoothly as possible to keep Abby asleep. I always harbored the ridiculous hope that Abby could somehow remain peacefully asleep through all fifteen minutes of surface-street maneuvering until we reached our final destination. I would hold my breath and shift to neutral as silently as I could, drifting to a gentle stop at the first stoplight. And just as I would begin to think I had managed to keep the baby asleep, Isaac would burst out with something like, "Snack! Snack! SNACK!" Naturally, the next fifteen minutes would be filled with inconsolable wailing.

But, in spite of his follies and his fury at no longer being the center of the universe, Isaac generally tolerates his little sister. In fact, on a rare occasion, he has even been observed to show affection, little-boy style. Soon after Abby came home, I looked up to notice a pile of Isaac's favorite dinosaurs, Abby's head barely visible above the mound. Isaac sat next to her with a broad, gaping grin. He actually wanted to share his toys with his new little baby! He's slowly adapting to this shared universe and he shows signs of being a good and gentle big brother. Change can be tough, but he's working his way through it. I think he might even love his Abby-Sister.

A PROMISE

"For I am the Lord, I do not change" (Malachi 3:16a).

A PRAYER

Lord, we are a family in the midst of great change. We are seeing relationships change, attitudes change, and familiar routines change. We are so thankful to remember that there is One who does not change. We praise You for being constant during our transition so that we have an anchor to keep us from being swept away by our shifting circumstances.

Metamorphosis

A PERSPECTIVE

Abby spent her first six weeks as all newborns do: eating, pooping, sleeping, eating, pooping, sleeping. Meanwhile, below the radar of my distracted attention, something strange and sinister began to take place in my first-born child.

No one warned me during my first pregnancy that my baby would eventually grow into an extraordinarily altered being. I'm sure the experienced mothers in my life watched with irony as I naively painted and fluffed Isaac's nursery. They were probably laughing to themselves at the thought of what that once-tidy nursery would look like eighteen months later. I had no clue what was coming.

I remember when Isaac was around eight months old and I invited my friend Melissa to come visit with her two little boys. Since Isaac was at the stage of playing quietly at my feet, he really did not need much to entertain him. His small toy shelf was typically neatly organized. I even took the time to arrange the blocks on his toy train so that they spelled out "I-S-A-A-C-S—T-R-A-I-N." Awww, how cute, right!? He didn't actually *play* with the train. We just used it as decoration. At most, maybe I'd pull a few blocks down for him to

24

chew on and then neatly restack them later when he was finished. What a schmuck!

Well, when Melissa's boys came over for their first visit, I was caught quite off guard by their quick and thorough destruction of *my* organized toy shelf. Within minutes, every delicately arranged toy on the small shelf was scattered throughout my entire house. I thought, "These boys are wild! They're crazy! They're out of control!" Now, these are two of the sweetest and cutest little boys in the world (and Melissa is one of the best, most disciplined, and present mothers in the world) and yet in my sheltered new-mother mind, I thought the boys were the equivalent of two small but destructive wind storms. Today, I am forced to admit that I have my own little tornado. How could I know this was going to happen?! I was *so* not prepared for this!

In fact, I think it would be much nicer if every baby came with a warning label: "WARNING: this low-maintenance, immobile, snuggly humanoid infant will one day, much sooner than you expect, become a whining, yelling, laughing, singing, running, climbing, throwing, hitting, dumping, exploring, and rapidly growing humanoid *toddler*. Buyer beware!" If you haven't yet experienced this metamorphosis with your own infant, I assure you this description is quite accurate. You can even ask my almost-two-year-old son and he'll confirm it by looking you in the eye and then licking you on the cheek.

Right under my nose, my child subtly morphed from something gentle and Jello-like into something completely unfamiliar. Although still cute, my altered child has the combined destructive capacity of eighteen jackhammers and a pair of dancing Sumo wrestlers. In fact, it's a good thing that I wasn't issued this strange new life-form, also known as "toddler," right off the bat at the hospital. If they had tried to send me home with a toddler, I would have simply denied the fact that I just gave birth. "What baby?" I would have exclaimed, eyeing the toddler suspiciously. "That's not my baby! I was just here for a vision test."

Isaac's metamorphosis occurred gradually and as his second birthday drew closer, I was left amazed at the new boy-child that was growing in my home. These toddlers come with a whole new set of rules:

Rule #1: The parent is never right
Something seemingly as harmless as offering the child a toy or snack can prove fatal:

Mommy: Isaac, would you like an apple?

Isaac: No, I don't want to.

Mommy: Okay, Mommy will eat it then.

Isaac: NO! My apple!

Mommy: Okay, here you go!

Isaac: I don't want to.

Mommy: That's fine. I'll just put it on the counter for later.

Isaac: My apple. My apple!

Mommy: It's okay. You can have it!

Isaac: NO!!!!!

And so on. Tears are always involved in such dangerous exchanges and no matter what I do, it is clearly wrong.

Rule #2: The toddler is incapable of stillness

If you pick Isaac up under his armpits and hold him in the air, his legs keep pumping in "air-bicycle" circles until you set him down again to zoom off at top speed. I'm pretty sure that if the government could find a way to tap into toddler energy, they could supply the entire country with electricity for months from just one kid.

Rule #3: The toddler must whine at all times

Having grown out of toddlerdom several years ago myself, I no longer speak fluent whine. Therefore, I find myself correcting all morning long: "Can you think of a better way to say that?" "Please ask again nicely." "If you don't stop whining, Mommy's going to have to move to Alaska."

Rule #4: The toddler must invade every square inch of the parent's personal space in new and increasingly violent ways

Sometimes it's: pull Mommy's hair in an effort to scale her back, Everest-style. Other times, the boy springs suddenly from a piece of furniture onto my lap, in joyous attack-mode. His hands must always be poking, prodding, pinching, and pulling at me.

Rule #5: The toddler must talk nonstop

This nonstop chatter occurs from the time they wake up until the time they fall into blessedly silent slumber each night. All those days of anxiety about whether the child would ever learn to speak are long gone. Now Momma just wonders whether the child will ever be quiet again! Isaac will talk even if he has absolutely nothing to say:

Isaac: Mommy. Mom. Mommy. Moooooom!

Mommy: What!

Isaac: You're my mom.

Mommy: Yes, and you're my baby boy.

Isaac: Mommy. Mom. Mommy. Moooooom!

Mommy: What!?!

Isaac: I'm a giant robot.

Mommy: Okaaay.

Forgive me for my lack of enthusiasm. It's just that we've been having this same conversation multiple times an hour for the past three months.

Rule #6: (optional) Some toddlers must be extremely clingy
This one is not as universal as the above-mentioned rules. Some toddlers I know would be perfectly content if their moms dropped them off for a week to be cared for by a family of wooly mammoths. However, clinginess is nonetheless a hurdle for many toddler parents.

In spite of all my efforts, Isaac still refuses to play independently, preferring instead to be right underfoot. It amazes me that so much love and aggravation can be wrapped up together in one small package. It's like this: imagine you've recently purchased the most beautiful dress, wanting to wear it every day because it brings you so much joy. But as much as you love it, your new dress has a problem –it has a major case of static cling. So you wear it around every day, loving it and treasuring it, all the while wishing there was some product that could keep that gorgeous fabric from creeping up your legs before you trip over it and fall flat on your face. Yes, I'm comparing my son to a dress and yes, he's got a really bad case of static cling!

When I take a good look at my toddler-child and realize how much he's changed in the last year, I can't help but think to myself, "Who is this strange child? I ordered an infant...what happened to it?" But, sometimes this thought is actually sprinkled with a dash of pride. I'm not sure how my child grew from nineteen inches to a lanky thirty-six. I'm not sure how he came to be capable of sitting there completing a wooden puzzle without my help. Somehow, without my noticing, by small, incremental changes, my baby has become a fully functioning child. Is this a good thing? Time will tell.

A PROMISE

"...Let the little children come to Me, and do not forbid them; for of such is the kingdom of God" (Mark 10:14).

A PRAYER

Lord, it is difficult at times for me to imagine You actually welcoming my wild child into Your presence. What would You do if he licked You on the cheek or pulled Your hair and wiggled away laughing? My guess is that you are able to see his pure heart in spite of his antics. You shower him with love no matter how contrary his attitude can be. Help me to see his heart as You do and to love him unconditionally.

More than My Hands Full

A PERSPECTIVE

With two kids, I have *more* than my hands full. Sure, I've got *two* kids and *two* hands. The math adds up. So why is this harder than it seems like it should be? Well, if all I had to do during the day was hold the kids, my two hands would suffice. But somehow they also have to be fed and cleaned and entertained and my two hands are just about the limits of our resources.

This morning, I decided Isaac would get to play in the backyard splash pool. I slathered him with sunscreen, changed him into his swim diaper, hauled out the pool, attached the hose, and sat down to hold Abby. Then I got back up again to get the chalk Isaac was throwing into the water and sat back down to hold Abby. Then I got back up to help Isaac open the toy box and get some toys and sat back down to hold Abby, who at that point had started to fuss. Then I got back up AGAIN because Isaac, just ten minutes after we came outside, wants to go "inside please, inside please, inside pleeeeeeeeeease!"

Later in the day, as I prepare for dinner, Isaac stands on a chair eating the veggies I have just chopped and spreading the grated cheese all over the counter as he stuffs it into his mouth. According to custom, he has been "helping" me cook by "mixing" and "mashing" anything he can get his hands on.

Meanwhile, Abby has been patiently sitting in her bouncy seat (again) for half an hour and is now getting antsy. As I go to pick her up, Isaac is leaning tippy-toe over the edge of the chair he's standing on, trying to reach the knife I left just out of his reach on the counter. I stop unbuckling Abby and rush back to catch Isaac before he falls or reaches the knife or both. Abby, now frustrated that she was not rescued on my first attempt, starts to cry and Isaac starts whining in a broken-record pattern because he wants to "chop please, chop please, chop please, chop please, chop pleeeeeeeeeease!"

While Abby works up to a wail in her bouncy seat, I hold Isaac's hands, trying to make eye contact, and explain in a pseudo-calm voice, "Isaac, I appreciate you saying 'please' but you cannot chop. Only mommies and daddies can chop because it's dangerous. Here, why don't you help peel the corn?" He stops fighting me once I hand him the corn.

I return again to my poor, neglected Abby. Her face is red and she's starting to sweat. I gently pick her up, turning around to see that Isaac has already "peeled" the corn, leaving the husk all over the floor. He's currently taking bites out of the uncooked corn and he's made an impromptu toupee out of the corn's "hair."

Squatting on the floor next to where Isaac is now sitting, I try to get him stop eating raw corn and pick up the mess he's made as Abby slumps over one of my arms, head dangling precariously. After the past five minutes (yes, that was just five minutes-worth of charming interaction with my expressive children), my blood pressure has risen to code blue levels and I've sprouted eight more gray hairs.

I call my husband to see when he's coming home. He doesn't answer his phone. Hopefully that means he's on his way already. Abandoning my meager attempt at cooking, I plug Isaac in to the TV so I can nurse Abby. While I'm nursing, my phone rings. Of course I've left it on the kitchen counter. So, with Abby struggling to keep her grasp on my nipple, I wobble over to the kitchen just in time to miss the last ring of the phone. It was Adel so I call him back. He's still at work and won't be able to leave for another hour.

Somebody save me, somebody save me pleeeeeeeeease!

By the time Adel gets home two hours later, I'm grumpy and exhausted. Dinner is now a comical affair. With one child, Adel and I could take turns eating. Usually Adel would hold or tend to Isaac while I gulped down my food so his dinner wouldn't get too cold. Now with two kids, no one gets to eat. One of us is holding Abby while the other is feeding and maintaining Isaac (he requires a lot of maintenance). Somehow we survive the meal, toss down a few cold bites and move on to The Bedtime Routine.

At Isaac's bedtime, Abby is fed up with the bouncy seat and infant swing that she's been confined to for a greater part of the day. She insists on being held. Adel sways with Abby while I wrestle Isaac into his jammies, read him a book or four, fetch him his new favorite toy (changes every five minutes), get him another drink of milk, hold him for the bedtime prayer, and finally put him down in his crib to sleep (yes, he's still in a crib because I'm not about to start *that* battle).

As I gently close his door, I breathe a sigh of relief. I've made it through the day at last! Oh, wait. No I haven't. Abby's still awake. She stays awake for the next three hours. Adel and I take turns putting her down and picking her up until finally she stays asleep.

Now, I feel torn. I see the needs of my house. Toys scattered everywhere, the dishwasher to empty and fill yet again, diapers overflowing the pail. There are emails to write, phone calls to make, bills to pay, three-foot-tall weeds to pull...but...I...need...sleep. Anything outside of survival will have to wait for another day.

A PROMISE

"My flesh and my heart fail; but God is the strength of my heart and my portion forever" (Psalm 73:26).

A PRAYER

God, I am tired. I know that You are my strength in the daily struggles I face as a new mother of two. I pray that you would help me endure minutes that seem as long as days and days that seem to last a lifetime.

TV vs Reality

A PERSPECTIVE

Little Abby seems to nurse approximately every hour and a half for three hours straight. I know that's not even mathematically possible but that's the way it seems. It's especially challenging to nurse so often when I have a toddler who remains constantly in motion, often with the intent of inflicting personal harm to his precious little self. As a result of this challenge, like it or not, the television has become one of my nearest and dearest friends. When I need to nurse the newborn for an extended period of time, it is easiest to turn on the TV and let the toddler experience life the couch-potato way. The only thing is, I've been affronted lately with the stark contrast between life as I know it and the fantasy world of television family life.

I recently finished watching a children's program with Isaac. It's about a sweet little four-year-old boy whose eternally calm and nurturing parents take him on an unending variety of educational down-home adventures. They're all way too sweet to be real and the whole scenario makes me want to jump into the television set and slap the entire family. I would grab their round cartoon faces and scold, "Wake up, people! This is not how it really works!"

For one thing, the television-child *never* whines. I understand that the network is attempting to model good behavior to their child-viewers, but as a realistic parent (perhaps particularly vulnerable and overwhelmed at this moment), I ooze sarcasm as I watch this kid "please" and "thank-you" his way sweetly through everything. You *never* see him in time-out or being disciplined for bad behavior.

That is because he is *never* bad. When left to his own devices, the boy entertains himself. Instead of groveling at his mother's feet, the preferred activity of my own active son, this child actually has the gumption to think up a creative activity which he can accomplish independently. Often this involves the use of a few, select toys that seem to be the only toys in the center of an immaculately clean room. This child *never* gets bored with these few toys and absolutely *never* takes one of those toys and abandons it willy-nilly on the floor in a completely different location. I'm sure he would stare aghast at the behavior of my two-year-old son.

Clearly, the television child gets his flawless persona from his parents. His mother is always *calmly* feeding his baby sister, or *calmly* cooking a nice three course meal, or *calmly* folding the laundry. His mother *never* yells or even raises her voice. While preparing the picnic lunch and loading up the car for her family she *never* looses her patience and yells, "Would you leave me alone for ONE SECOND so I can get everything ready for our PEACEFUL-BLOOMING- FAMILY PICNIC?!"

I'm sure she remains so well-adjusted herself because of the gentle handiness of her loving husband. He is so efficient that common household chores, like mowing the lawn, washing the car, or filing paperwork, only have to be done approximately once a year, when they serve an educational purpose for his son. Naturally, this clears up much of his time for other enlightening adventures such as fishing trips, camping, hiking, and sledding. The only clue to the resourceful patron's means of employment is that he occasionally enters or exits the home bearing a briefcase.

The father is *never* stressed about taxes, the mortgage, or the daily grind of work. The mother *never* despairs over her unending task of nurturing, tending, and providing. The boy *never* acts out just to get attention. The baby sister *never* cries, poops, or barfs. It's a wonderful life.

My life, however, is not at all like that. I am currently a stressed out, disorganized mess. My husband is in way over his head trying to balance my many needs with the demands of his new job. My daughter passionately insists on nursing every hour and a half for three hours straight. And my son...oh, my son...well, to put it gently, he has several idiosyncrasies that, when applied with the relentless consistency of Chinese water torture, can really drive me insane.

The disparity between the fantasy of the TV family and my own life makes me feel like a bitter old nag. I'm pretty sure I'm developing an attitude problem (okay, so maybe I had an attitude problem before this point, but who's to say for sure?). All I know is, I'm jealous of a cartoon family. That's really sad.

I need my chocolate. Just shoot it directly into my veins!

A PROMISE

"Search me, O God, and know my heart; try me, and know my anxieties; and see if there is any wicked way in me, and lead me in the way everlasting" (Psalm 139:23-24).

A PRAYER

Lord, when I see or hear idealism in regards to raising children, it is often the kind of life I would *like* to provide for my kids. However, the images are often frustratingly far from my own chaotic reality. Please help me to strive for excellence as a parent while maintaining Your heart of grace toward myself. Thank You for loving me even when I do not live up to my own expectations (or Yours).

Houseful of Memories

A PERSPECTIVE

I have never been one to become sentimental over a home. This is probably because when I was growing up I never lived in one for more than a few years. It's easy to say goodbye to a home when you are quite accustomed to packing up and moving on. We never had to leave behind a lifetime of memories. Then after Adel and I married, we lived in one starter home after the next, none of which begged for emotional attachment (mold-decay, termite infestations, noisy neighbors, and two-hour commutes don't lend themselves to sad goodbyes). But here in our new house, I am beginning to understand how one's heart can be deeply rooted into one's home.

We moved to Texas just a few months before Abby was born. In our new state, housing prices were phenomenally lower than in our native Southern California. As a result, we had a tough decision to make:

Option #1: buy a starter home that would still be a giant step up from our small Anaheim condominium. Keep this home for a few years, pocketing our extra income, and then buy our dream home later when we could better afford it.

Option #2: stretch our income as far as it would go to buy our dream home now and stay here indefinitely.

Well, we found our dream home pretty quickly:

Us: Seriously? We can afford *that*?

Our loan officer: Yes, but according to these figures you won't be able to afford anything else, including food and diapers!

Us: Yeah, but we can afford it? Sweet!

Okay, so the decision wasn't *that* tough. Since we had already been accustomed to stretching our income to afford our tiny California condo, we decided to continue along our same tight budget in order to afford this spacious new home. So in lieu of diapers, we will continue to use rolled-up gym socks and duct tape. You do what you gotta do, right?

This house has everything I ever wanted in a home. At least it has everything on my *grown-up* wish list. As a kid, I wanted some pretty ridiculous things like an entire room made of trampoline and an indoor circus complete with cotton candy vendors. As an adult, I will settle for the niceties of modern living like reliable plumbing and light switches that actually are wired to *turn something on* when you flick them. This house has enough rooms for both my kids to have their own, something that never would have happened for us in California. It also has lots of open space to play. I was so excited on the night we first moved in that I made snow angels on the carpet in our empty bedroom. I felt like we finally had room to breathe and stretch out our arms.

Now that we've settled into this new house, I'm finally beginning to understand those sappy television shows where a family is all broken up about a house that they're leaving after so many years.

And it's not because this house is so great that I couldn't stand to leave it. I can relate to those house-loving people because for the first time, I live in a home that I don't intend to vacate for many, many years. I hope this will be the place where we store a lifetime of memories.

Soon after we moved in, as I sat watching Isaac play, I had a vision of our life to come:

In my vision, I was fifteen years older than I am now and still living in this house. (I looked great, by the way.) *I stood in the living room, watching Isaac, a tall and lanky teenager, descend the stairs.* (Okay, maybe he won't be that tall, if you take a good look at his parents, but this is my vision!) *Isaac, this tall, lanky teenager with dark stubble on his chin, was heading out of the house for his last day of high school before going off to college. As the "future me" watched this near-grown man, I had a flashback to our first days in this house. I remembered back to when Isaac was a toddler, scooting wildly up and down those same stairs and waddling in his crinkling, little diaper.*

Imagining this scenario, I felt a deep, sentimental pang as I thought of that same staircase trodden with the footsteps of my child now, tomorrow, and every day until the day he strikes out on his own. Then to think of baby *Abby* growing up here too was just too much to bear. I got all misty-eyed at the thought of the memories we would make so quickly within the walls of our new home. This time with Isaac and Abby being so little, though often challenging and grueling, is also precious and something to be cherished. My hope is that years from now the familiar walls of this home where we've lived together for so long will flood us all with memories and remind us of how much we love each other and the life we share.

With a quavering voice, feeling a bit sheepish, I told Adel about my vision. Accustomed to my over-active imagination, my dear husband directed Isaac dryly, "Give your mommy a hug, Isaac. She's sad because you grew up too fast."

A PROMISE

"I thank my God upon every remembrance of you" (Philippians 1:3).

A PRAYER

Lord, thank You for this home and for the beautiful memories we are making within these walls. We hope, by Your mercy, to raise our children here and house a lifetime of remembrances.

Sleep Wars

A PERSPECTIVE

So, you think you have a "strong-willed child"? As my son's prominent personality began to dawn on me, I devoured Dr. James Dobson's book of that title. I'm pretty sure I have a story here that would get an approving nod from the long-suffering parents described in his book. I believe I'm part of a club, albeit not a very fun or popular one. You see, there are *parents* and then there are *parents of strong-willed children.* Dr. Dobson, check out this story of a strong-willed child:

(As a side note, this is *so* not a "how-to-get-your-child-to-sleep" advice column. If I had known how to do it in the first place, this story would have never been written!)

Stage 1: Bedtime Battle | Victor: Mimi and Boppa

It happened soon after Abby was born, perhaps as a result of the changes occurring in Isaac's small, fragile world. When people would ask me how I was adjusting to having two kids, I would tell them, "I'm *so* tired." Naturally, they all assumed it was the newborn who was keeping me up at all hours of the night. But in reality, Abby slept great from day one. It was *Isaac* who was causing me so much trouble.

I realize that bedtime battles are not unusual for toddlers, who are looking to set their own rules and be their own boss, all at the mature age of two. We had experienced bedtime battles before this point, but nothing prepared us for the tyrannical will-power of our now two-year-old boy. We began to suspect that Isaac was secretly undergoing endurance training with the Navy Seals.

Each night at the conclusion of the bedtime routine, Isaac would start screaming. We're talking beyond whining and cries for help. This was full-out, bloody-murder, writhing-body, throw-up inducing, hysterical, raging screams. I moved his bedtime an hour later and tried installing a nightlight, singing songs, uninstalling the nightlight, rocking him to sleep, rubbing his back, reinstalling the nightlight, and even laying down next to him in his crib (desperation!). I also tried to cultivate his affections toward a stuffed bunny as a comfort object. He liked the bunny but I guess not enough to sleep without a fight. All my attempts to get him to sleep willingly ended in frustration as his screaming began again the minute I would attempt to tiptoe out of the room. As much as I wanted to keep him from crying, I could not ignore the fact that I now have *another* child who also needs me and, oh yeah, *I* occasionally need to get some sleep too.

Finally, after weeks of trying to compromise and wearing myself out, I told him that he was going to have to fall asleep on his own, no matter what. After the bedtime routine, I wrenched his monkey-death grip from around my neck and forced his flailing limbs into his crib with as much tenderness as one can muster when fighting against a raging toddler. I called out "I love you!" over his screams of protestation and I walked out the door. I did not go back in because I knew if I did I would be suckered into just one more thing. First, "Mommy come over here." Then, "Mommy pick me up." Then, "Mommy take me downstairs." Then, "Mommy buy me a space shuttle." We had been through all that before. So this time the closest

I approached was for a periodic glance through the crack in the door to make sure he was unharmed during his assault on the air.

That night he kept it up for *three straight hours*. When he finally became quiet, around 11:00pm I crept in to check on him. To my surprise, he was still standing in his bed. His head was resting on the top rail of his crib. Although his eyes were closed, he was still upright. His exhausted body could fight sleep no longer, but his determined will was too strong to just give up and lay down. So I watched him, time after time, as his knees buckled under his sleeping body, snapping him awake for a moment just in time to straighten back up again. He never opened his eyes. It was like when someone falls asleep sitting up on an airplane and their head keeps bobbing up and down. The head-dropping motion wakes them up just enough to pick their head back up again and start the whole process anew.

As I watched him, I tearfully thought of how sad I was that he was so stubborn to fight something that he needed almost as much as food and air. I wanted desperately to gently lay him down so he could sleep, but I was too fearful that if I did, he would wake up and start screaming all over again. So I stood in the doorway for ten minutes, watching to see what would happen. When nothing changed and he kept buckling and unbuckling his knees, I finally decided I had better try to get some sleep myself. Twenty minutes later, the screaming began afresh with renewed vigor. My guess is his tired legs finally gave out on him, letting him plop down on his mattress, which startled him awake.

At this point, after the three hours of screaming I had already endured, and then watching him attempt to sleep standing up, I could not take it any longer. I caved. I buckled. I conceded the battle to the one who wanted to win even more than I did. I ran upstairs, scooped him up, and carried him into my bed. He fell asleep instantly in my arms and remained content until just before dawn when he decided it was time to wake up.

After that, Isaac slept in my bed for a few weeks. Now, Adel and I have never been inclined to favor a "family bed." We like our space and our privacy and our relationship to each other far too much to have a child elbowing his way between us on a regular basis. But for a short time, we could see no other solution. Naturally, Isaac would refuse to go to sleep until we did. So we would all climb in bed at around nine o'clock. Then we were bombarded all night long with knees, feet, elbows, and hands, reaching out to bonk us for assurance that we were still there. After a week or so of this, Adel began to threaten sleeping in the guest bed.

Thankfully for our marriage and my sanity, the time came to attend the Michigan wedding of our friend Liz. Needing a break from Isaac's tyranny, we opted to leave him with Mimi and Boppa. Although we had been nervous about how he would do there, the little stinker miraculously went right to bed for his grandparents! We praised the Lord deeply when he transitioned back to his own bed after our trip.

Stage 2: Wake-Time Battle | **Victor: Mommy**

The battle then became about wake up time. He would willingly go to bed every night at eight o'clock only to wake up screaming at seven o'clock. Then he would wake up at six thirty; then six o'clock; then five forty-five; then five thirty; then five fifteen... It wasn't exactly to the minute like that but it got to the point where I could pretty much predict a ten to fifteen minute earlier wake up call than the day before. When the screaming started *before* five in the morning, I would attempt to communicate that it was too early to get up. "The sun isn't even up yet," I would explain, as if he cared.

Finally, after weeks of eating breakfast in the dark of night (while still waking up nightly to nurse Abby), I was so exhausted that I decided it had to be *him* or *me*. This is a terrible conclusion for a momma to come to but I was one worn out momma. One night as I laid him in his crib I told him, "I'll see you when the sun comes up."

44

The next morning, when he started screaming at four-thirty-something, I turned off the monitor and went back to sleep. I had set my alarm for six o'clock and when I woke up, I turned the monitor back on. He was still screaming but *I* sure felt better and I went to get him right away. After a week or so of this, the monitor began to be silent when I turned it back on at six o'clock. Then, he stopped waking up at four in the morning, and just gave in and slept until six o'clock too. Yay!

Stage 3: Naptime Battle | Victor: Isaac

Great, you must be thinking to yourself. *So finally he stopped fighting and just slept like he is supposed to.* And oh, how I wish you were right in thinking this! But, remember, he had been secretly training with the Navy Seals and is iron-willed. He merely shifted his strategy. Now the battle lines were drawn over the afternoon nap.

As his night-sleep had done weeks before, his naptime began to creep shorter and shorter. It finally settled at thirty minutes. He would go down for his nap willingly, exhausted from his early rising in the morning. Then, exactly half an hour later, he would wake up screaming. Again, for a while I attempted to force him to get more sleep. His screams told me he clearly wasn't getting enough. But there's only so long you can keep a child in his bed in the afternoon before it gets to be too close to his bedtime to matter anymore. So it was me who did the giving in this time and for months Isaac napped for exactly thirty minutes and woke up screaming daily. It was so accurate I could set my watch by it.

This period of time was less emotionally challenging than the nighttime and early morning battles had been. But it was difficult to be so strapped for "me" time. Before Abby, Isaac's naptime had been the time when I would do my quiet time, my chores, my writing, my email and phone calls. But with Isaac only napping for thirty minutes and Abby adding her own needs to my laundry-list, I pretty much accomplished only an intense sense of panic as I tried to accomplish something, *anything*, before the screaming began.

45

Stage 4: Peacetime | Victor: Everyone

Months later, he began to nap better once again and even began "sleeping in" on some days until seven o'clock! In all my days as a parent so far, those "sleep war" days were my most difficult. Throughout the entire conflict with Isaac I was still waking up one or two times each night to feed little Abby. Although she would go right back to sleep quite willingly, I found myself completely exhausted by juggling the different sleep issues of my two young children. The sleeplessness of course made everything else harder to handle. And if my actions seem heartless, you must know that I shed nearly as many tears as the boy did. I shudder when I think of those trying days, hating that I had to battle my own son so fiercely for something that he needs for his own good. (And yes, Mom, I realize the irony that I was a difficult child myself and so am probably just reaping what I sowed!)

A PROMISE

"My son, keep your father's command, and do not forsake the law of your mother. Bind them continually upon your heart; tie them around your neck. When you roam, they will lead you; when you sleep, they will keep you; and when you awake, they will speak with you" (Proverbs 6:20-22).

A PRAYER

God, I pray that You will give me the strength to fight for what I know my children need, even against their own desires. I pray that I will know which battles are worth fighting and which battles I need to let go. Mostly, I pray that my strong-willed child knows in the end how much I love him and that when he grows up he will have more memories of my love than of our battles.

Control, or the Lack Thereof

As I lay here close to tears, trying to snuggle a wiggling Isaac back to sleep after his frustratingly short afternoon nap, I finally realize what God has been trying to teach me in these past few months: **I am not in control here**.

It's hard to admit, but my beloved toddler is slowly driving me insane. Sometimes, I feel like a clock being wound up too tightly. If I don't find a way to unwind, and fast, something's going to snap. At other times, my interaction with Isaac reminds me of a dentist, chipping harmlessly away at a tooth until…WHAM…he hits a nerve. After hours of whine-correction, personal-space-invasion, or non-stop conversation, sometimes I suddenly explode. I snap. I growl. I bark. I say something mean that I wish I didn't say.

Although I've often wished for an all-inclusive guide to parenting, I'm pretty sure there is not yet one in existence. However, if there were an "official parenting guidebook," such as *The Imbecile's Guide to Flawless Parenting*, I have no doubt that it would say something like this:

Maintain your composure and loving patience with your children in all situations. It is acceptable to give your toddler consequences for his actions. However, this must not be done in anger. You, the parent, the one in charge, should maintain controlled responses to the most vexing circumstances. Wait a minute. Who are you kidding? You can't even control the direction the water spins in your toilet! What makes you think that you can control your child's behavior or your responses to him? Isn't there someone else around who's better qualified for this job of parenting than you? No? You're the only one available? Well then, best wishes.

Perhaps part of the reason I often find it so difficult to curtail my emotional responses is that I'm not getting the rest I need (I know, big surprise). We're still engaged in the grueling sleep war with Isaac that began soon after Abby joined the family. At all hours I find myself battling, coaxing, pleading, cajoling, bribing...anything to get that little rascal to sleep! But I am learning that the amount of sleep my children get is yet another thing that is far beyond my control.

At naptime, I have just put Isaac down in his bed. Abby's asleep in the swing. I slink under my covers to rest after a frustrating morning and a much-too-short night's sleep. As my eyelids close, I hear Abby starting to wriggle in the swing. Knowing it's only a matter of time before she starts to fuss and cry, I desperately try *willing* myself to sleep. If I were my husband I would be asleep already but, tired as I am, I can't sleep under this kind of pressure. *I* don't have an "off" switch. I lay here thinking about how I *should be sleeping* until I hear the inevitable cry. Thirty minutes later, Abby is nursed, changed, and rocked back to sleep. I collapse on the bed again to try once more to rest. But as my head settles back on the pillow, Isaac starts calling, "mommy please, mommy please, mommy please, mommy pleeeeeeeeeease!"

Some days like this are jam packed with "opportunities" for me to demonstrate self-control, gentleness, and patience. Others, although far more rare, pass relatively pleasantly and without testing my spirit. The one thing that remains consistent throughout all my days lately is the obvious acknowledgement that **I am not in control**. Not even a little bit.

A friend once gave me a wallet-sized card that had a picture of two penguins on it. One of the penguins is standing there with a giant orange fish stuck on his head. The other penguin remarks stoically, "Relax, God's in charge." I have come to the realization that, despite all my efforts to create order out of chaos, I am the penguin with the fish stuck on my head.

As a result of all of these factors, and many more, I am being forced to admit that at this time in my life, no amount of scheduling, planning, prepping, or effort is going to help me feel in control. I cannot force Isaac to sleep. I cannot grow an extra arm or be in three places at once. I cannot be all things to all people the way my children want me to be. There are times when one of them is just going to have to cry because I can't always meet both their needs simultaneously. Supermom does not exist, at least not in this house.

At the times when I feel at my wits' end, desperate for a cavalry that does not arrive, I find myself crying out to the Lord. I am not in control and I need someone bigger and greater than myself to be in control for me! Perhaps ironically, I have been too overwhelmed to even think about having a regular quiet time lately. Without my daily time set aside to spend with Him, I have been trying to make it on my own. I need to be depending on God, relying on His Holy Spirit and His written word, crying out to my Savior. My own strength is finite and fleeting. His is everlasting. I cannot raise my children without Him. Heck, I cannot even *survive* my children without Him!

A PROMISE

"Hear my cry, O God; attend to my prayer. From the end of the earth I will cry to You, when my heart is overwhelmed; Lead me to the rock that is higher than I" (Psalm 61:1-2).

A PRAYER

God, I need You. Sometimes it's easy for me to forget this. But right now is *not* one of those times. The daily struggle of parenting two very little children reminds me again and again how desperately I need You. My own strength is just not enough. Although I am often not here for You, I thank You for always being here for me!

Shopping Trip

A PERSPECTIVE

Abby is now two months old, so a small voice inside of me said this morning, "It's high time you go on a productive outing with your two children."

It didn't take me too long to discover that this was actually the voice of "Doom," the red horseman of the apocalypse. I'm sure of this because this particular horseman's goal is to wipe peace from the face of the earth. Here's how my shopping trip went:

10:08AM
- We pull into the Target parking lot
- Isaac contentedly watches Buzz Lightyear blow up robots on the DVD player
- Abby stares out the back window
- I'm full of vigor and enthusiasm for accomplishing my little errand

10:09AM
- I load both kids into the shopping cart
- Isaac sits cross-legged in the basket
- Abby's car seat clicks onto the handlebars of the cart

10: 11AM

- I enter Target, pushing the cart with both kids, list in hand
- Isaac immediately begins to show signs of revolt
- I dig out his snacks from the diaper bag to buy some time
- Abby starts to fuss
- I begin to think this was a bad idea

10:13AM

- Isaac contentedly snacks on goldfish in the basket
- Abby fusses loud enough to alert customers ten aisles away of our approach
- I try letting her suck on my finger but it does no good
- Still, I press on past four or five aisles, hoping Abby will settle down

10:15AM

- Abby, face red and strained, mouth gaping, tiny fits flailing, wails angrily to inform me that she's not getting her way
- Old women begin staring at me and my face turns white with anxiety
- I'm afraid I will soon be asked to leave for disturbing the peace
- With my cart still empty, I turn around and retreat out the door

10:16AM

- As soon as the cart hits daylight, Abby stops crying
- I get to the car, thinking perhaps I should go back and try it again

10:17AM

- Abby seems fine now so I return through the doors of Target, list in hand

10:18AM

- Abby's wail can now be heard in Antarctica

- The same old women now scowl at me, the disapproval on their faces broadcasting, "What kind of mother drags a poor, neglected infant along on a shopping trip?...and why isn't she wearing a cap on her head...She'll catch a cold!" (It doesn't matter what season it is, old women always want babies to wear caps on their heads)
- Isaac has finished his goldfish and is starting to get antsy again, threatening to disembowel my diaper bag and scatter the contents to the winds
- I melt into a mortified heap in the middle of the first aisle before regaining the strength to push the cart back outside
- As I retreat, I remain fearful that the old ladies will follow me, beating me over the head with their large purses

10:19AM

- Once again, as soon as the cart hits daylight, Abby stops crying
- This time I will not be fooled and we return to the car anyway
- She does not fuss again the rest of the morning (stinker!)

10:32AM

- We are back in the safety and solitude of our home
- Isaac is gleefully making a mess out of the playroom
- I don't care anymore that I couldn't complete my errand
- I'm just glad to be home again where old ladies don't scare me pallid and my personal chaos is not on display
- Abby is nursing contentedly as if to say, "Silly mommy, you don't need to *do* anything. The only thing you need to accomplish right now is *me!*"

A PROMISE

"Behold, children are a heritage from the Lord, the fruit of the womb is a reward. Like arrows in the hand of a warrior, so are the children of one's youth" (Psalm 127:3-4).

53

A PRAYER

Lord, I thank You for the gift of my children. Even in my most challenging moments as a mom, I am aware of the wonderful blessing You have given me in my children. Teach me to focus on the blessings instead of the struggles and to find joy in doing nothing more than raising my children.

Important Phone Call

A PERSPECTIVE

Just before Abby was born, I sent out letters to publishers regarding my first book. I waited for months to hear back from any of them. Finally, I received a phone call. I was thrilled. Here I was, talking on the phone with a publisher who was interested in my book about new motherhood!

Unfortunately, he caught me at a bad moment. While I conversed with the publisher regarding solid family values and godly motherhood, *my family* was completely falling apart! Just as the phone rang, I had been buckling two-month-old Abby into the bouncy seat so I could put away the laundry in the closet. Isaac was circling my legs in his usual destructive pattern, pulling all the shoes off the shoe rack as he passed by.

When I answered the phone, things were relatively peaceful in my home, but every mom knows that it only takes a quick phone conversation to fuel child-induced mayhem. So, as I answered questions on my thoughts about wisdom for young mothers, Abby began to wriggle and fuss in the bouncy seat. She was getting sleepy and wanted to be held. Thinking this phone conversation couldn't possibly last too long, and bursting with excitement about the prospects of getting published, I opted to leave her for a while so I could finish my interview in peace. After all, even if she was unhappy, I knew she was safe.

From that point on Abby's cries grew in volume and intensity as I moved farther and farther away from my crying infant so that her cries wouldn't be audible to my prospective publisher. I was determined to convince this guy that I am a *good mother* and that my book on motherhood was worthy of publishing. And I was even willing to make this point at the expense of my own children.

Meanwhile, Isaac's antics, left unchecked by me in my eager oblivion, were growing increasingly hazardous. At the climax of his frolicking, he climbed up on the umbrella stroller I had left in the living room, and stood on the flimsy cloth seat. I, of course, had no idea what he was up to, since I had barricaded myself in the laundry room to escape the din of my children. Abruptly, my conversation was interrupted by a crash and a toddler-sized wail (in natural dissonance to Abby's infant-sized wail still ringing from the bedroom).

I hurriedly excused myself from the phone call, telling the publisher that my son had just fallen down and needed my help. (I left out the part about my non-attention leading to his fall from the umbrella stroller). I put down the phone, comforted Isaac, handed him a snack, and returned to wrap up the increasingly exasperating interview. When the conversation finally ended, all was quiet in my home again. Isaac was still eating his snack and Abby was…hmmm…what *was* Abby doing?

Anxiously, I crept back into the bedroom, hoping she was still okay. That phone call took a lot longer than I anticipated. To my relief, she was peacefully asleep, although the means of getting there were none too peaceful.

Thank the Lord we all made it through those ten minutes. In the end, I opted to self publish my book on new motherhood. The publisher, who turned out to be the only one interested, was asking too much from me. He would give me my "big break" but he would also own me for life. Not the deal I was hoping for. Besides, how much could that publisher, expecting a mother to have a lengthy conversation in the midst of her chaos, possibly know about motherhood?

It was retrospection that made me see the irony of the situation: how I, in the very act of trying to convince someone else of my motherly qualifications, made my children the lowest priority. My children, being resilient and tender-hearted, forgave my momentary hypocrisy and now thrive again in my (mostly) undivided attention.

A PROMISE

"Let love be without hypocrisy. Abhor what is evil. Cling to what is good" (Romans 12:9).

A PRAYER

God, You know that I don't always have the right priorities or make the right decisions. Often my children are the ones who suffer the results of my selfishness and hypocrisy. Help me to follow You in the midst of every situation and to choose the path and the priorities that I know You would want for me and for my kids.

Uber-Grandparents

A PERSPECTIVE

Isaac and Abby's grandparents are a force to be reckoned with. Mimi and Boppa come from a rare breed of grandparent known as "uber-grandparents." You may be lucky enough to have an uber-grandparent in your family, in which case you will be able to relate to this entry with enthusiastic head nods. If not, you may suddenly find yourself in favor of cloning so that we can mass-produce such devoted beings.

To be an uber-grandparent, one must meet three requirements:

First, uber-grandparents must be *doting* and *attentive*:

My mom spent much of her oxygen in the spring of 2005 making it clear to my sister and me that she could *not* be expected to drop everything in her life just to help take care of the new grandbabies at a moment's notice. She has since proven herself to be quite willing to drop everything in her life just to help take care of the grandbabies, although she does insist on two or even *three* moments notice.

Furthermore, Mimi worked very hard to lure my sister and me into moving our families from California to Texas so that she would be close enough to her kids and grandkids. She makes her "incentives" so *obvious* and calculated that one can not possibly accuse her of manipulation as one might with a parent who is *sneaky* and calculated. I have lightheartedly made this accusation several times, to which she has replied with a sly chuckle, "I *know*. Aren't I *terrible?*" We all nod in unison but deep down we're truly thankful that her efforts to draw us closer in proximity have brought us some extra pairs of helping hands. Oh, and we of course also enjoy the quality time with Mimi and Boppa that comes with living closer too!

In addition, my dad has instincts far beyond that of a normal grandfather. Upon seeing one of his daughters over-run by the demands of her children, a *normal* grandfather will pop open a bottle of beer in order to sit back and laugh at the comical scene. My dad, like the other *uber*-grandfathers in this world, will instead pop open a bottle of beer and then scoop up the children and take them off on an adventure to somewhere exciting like the mailbox or the birdfeeder.

He's not entirely to be trusted, often nearly bonking their tiny heads on the stucco walls outside or failing to notice their small cries for help until *after* their legs are overrun by fire ants. It seems to be under Boppa's "watchful" eye that catastrophic series of events occur in the lives of small children, such as falling into the pool and then, immediately after being fished out by a fully-clothed Boppa, getting stung by a bee. Nevertheless, our kids adore him and run to the door shouting "Boppa!" when he makes his entrance (which annoys the heck out of Mimi).

Secondly, an uber-grandparent must be *generous*:

My mom and dad were not always as well-to-do as they are these days. My mom loves to tell the story of when they were first married and so cash-poor that they would argue over whether bread or milk was a more important purchase. During that time, Mom once found a baby cockroach floating in their soup. After scooping it out discreetly, she proceeded to serve up the soup for them both and ate hers without complaint. They could not afford to waste good soup. Theirs is an American tale. They began humbly, worked hard and with integrity, and eventually became powerful and rich warlords. Okay, not warlords, and not all that powerful either, and compared to Bill Gates and other Jet Setters they are really not that rich. But, they have now amassed enough wealth to splurge on a regular basis and spoil those they love.

My mom, who spent her teenage years sewing her own dresses because she didn't have the cash to buy new ones, truly enjoys buying special treats for her kids and grandkids. If it weren't for my mother, my house would have no other decorations than the crumpled remnants of the posters that draped my dorm room walls (high school theater productions). I am especially grateful for her generosity during this time when all our financial resources are wrapped up in stretching to afford our first real house. Every time she comes, she brings items she just thought we might need (new cutting board, serving spoon, pack of paper towels, fruit fly trap…you know, something really necessary for survival). If I complain about something, her solution is often to take me out for some retail therapy. After I whined about how Isaac was driving me crazy while I cooked, she found a simple, inexpensive solution. For a time, while I cooked, Isaac would play with his magnetic refrigerator numbers and letters, naming them: "letter D, letter D, letter D," or counting them, "one, two, one, two, one, two…"

As for the uber-ness of Mimi and Boppa, as far as generosity is concerned, let's suffice it to say that I think they have more children's toys at their house than we do at ours. Mimi wants to make sure that our kids *want* to go there and it totally works. Isaac loves going to Mimi's house. She also wants us moms to want to go there too. So she makes it easy on us by having multiple versions of every kind of childcare device known to mankind. Of course, this works and we go there frequently. Sometimes I'm afraid we'll overstay our welcome and she'll finally kick us out. But that hasn't happened yet.

And Mimi is also very shrewd. She even wants her *son-in-laws* to want to go to her house. This is a little trickier. What in the world would make a son-in-law actually *want* to visit his mother-in-law on a regular basis? The trap, as baited by Mimi, is Wii. She installed a Wii and several games that they would like so they could play it upstairs in the game room while "watching" the kids. If it's been a long time since the last visit, Adel actually asks me, "When are we going back to Mimi's house?" The woman knows how to get what she wants.

The final quality an uber-grandparent must possess is a *slight case of insanity*:

That is the only way to explain why a grown person, who has just recently won his freedom from his own children, would willingly lure those grown children back to his home so that he could be a highly involved *grandparent* to his children's children. I guess it's similar to the way a woman forgets how much labor really hurts after she holds her new baby in her arms. My mom loves (and I mean *loves*) to tell me what a stinking rotten kid I was. My sister was the oldest —smart and well-behaved. Naturally, I spent the majority of my childhood trying to annoy everyone around me enough so that they would pay more attention to *me* than to *her*. My personality being quite similar to my Mom's caused us to butt heads roughly every thirty seconds. When we weren't actually in a fight, I would spend my time coming up with new ways to get on her nerves. To this day I am still quite good at it.

Why, just the other day at Walmart I found myself deliberately plunking her purse upside down in the cart, receiving a childish thrill out of knowing that she would fuss at me and we'd laugh about what a twerp I am. Mid-plunk, I realized that my behavior toward my mom was similar to Isaac's behavior toward me and I experienced a quick burst of insight into my son's soul. I played back in my mind the times when he frantically unrolls the toilet paper while I'm trying to quickly

61

use the toilet or when he throws all the contents of the diaper bag onto the floor, looking up with a mischievous grin as he awaits my response. He *loves* being a twerp to his mom just as much as I do to mine. Then I have to ask myself, why oh *why* would my mom invite *two* such twerps back into her beautifully-decorated, custom-fitted lifestyle? The only answer I can drum up is that she must be at least partially insane. Or her heart is as big as the Grinch's *after* he returns all the Christmas presents to the Whos down in Whoville and then carves the roast beast. Whatever the reason, I think my mom and dad should win a prize for being uber-grandparents of the year.

A PROMISE

"Children's children are the crown of old men, and the glory of children is their father" (Proverbs 17:6).

A PRAYER

Lord, thank you for the blessing of two such wonderful grandparents. I know they love me so much that their love overflows my cup and splashes blessings onto the heads of my children. I praise You for creating families to show each other little glimpses of what Your love is like.

Schlepping

Stay-at-home moms have become burdened with an unfortunate stereotype since the pearl-necked days of June Clever. I remember being about eight years old and trying to scrounge up a Halloween costume from the clothes we had around the house. For a while I settled on being a "housewife" such as I had seen other kids do in years past. It had to be one of the simplest and most recognizable costumes around: curlers in hair, blue mask on face, shabby bathrobe, and a pair of slippers. Simple, obvious, and quite funny (unless you happen to actually be a housewife!).

In the end I dressed as a "rich lady" in a black dress with a fake mink and costume jewelry. It was a stupid costume because everyone had to ask me what I was supposed to be. Most people assumed I was a dressed-up witch without a hat. I should have gone for the bathrobe. At least everyone would have recognized my costume on sight.

As for the stereotype of that bathrobed housewife with coffee mug in hand, I find myself these days in a bit of a quandary. Part of me doesn't want to believe that she exists. Not that I'm denying the existence of housewives, but does one really exist in such a bedraggled state? The rest of me, upon innocently glancing in the mirror, recognizes with shock that I have actually become her.

For example, one weekend Adel and I had planned to go visit my mom and dad. I wanted to pick him up from work so we could head out before rush hour. That afternoon I loaded the car with the two dogs and their leashes and food, and with the two kids and their sippy cups, snacks, diapers, wipes, change of clothes, travel beds, and pajamas…oh and a few necessities for Mommy and Daddy too. Can't go anywhere these days without sixteen travel bags.

I was wearing a pair of loose yoga pants and a shirt that was already smeared with snot and mashed bananas. My hair was pulled back in a ponytail that left big loose strands falling in my eyes. I wasn't exactly wearing a blue mask on my face but perhaps I actually would have been better off if I had.

Just as I pulled the over-loaded hatchback into the parking garage of Adel's workplace, I caught wind of that all-too-familiar poopy-diaper smell drifting up from the backseat. It was Abby, of course, but I was glad for the timing since it would have been impossible to change it once we were on the road. Since the hatchback was fully loaded, I laid Abby down on the front seat and struggled to keep her in one place while the dogs maneuvered to find a way past me and out to freedom beyond the door of the car.

Just as I turned, poopy diaper in hand, to find a trashcan, who should be walking my way? My arch enemy! My nemesis! Oh I know her well. She is the fashionable, clean, and well-put-together professional woman of the work-a-day world. She is the person *I* was *before* I had children. Her highlighted hair is neatly pulled back in an elegant twist, her manicured nails clutch delicately onto her sleek black portfolio, and her well-toned calves catch your eye from above the click-clack of her new leather heels. (Alright, so even when I was employed full-time, manicured nails were an occasional treat rather than a daily necessity. And, fine, I admit that I always opted for the comfort of flats over a classy pair of heels. And my hair only had highlights for the week of my wedding. But we're straying from the point, people! The point is, I used to feel at least a little attractive on a daily basis and this woman represented class and style so unattainable to me in my present state.)

As she passed, we sized each other up. (Okay, in truth it was probably only me who did the sizing up. She just smiled as she passed and was probably too busy thinking about her presentation for the important clients or her rendezvous with her secret lover. I, on the other hand, had nothing better to do than make comparisons.)

I imagined that this well-groomed woman took one look at my disorderly appearance and my overloaded junk-mobile and naturally assumed that I was some roving hillbilly setting up camp in the parking garage with my snot-nosed rug rats and my flea-ridden mongrels. I know, that's a bit extreme and perhaps I judged her a little too harshly. It is possible that she was able to look past the putrid diaper, the smear-stained shirt, the Raggedy Ann hairdo, and the dirty, overloaded car. It is possible that she looked at me and at my two darling children and longed for the day when she too could have a family of her own. Perhaps she'd be willing to give it all up (the manicures, the hair salon, the shopping sprees, the high-paying job…) if only she could stay home with a warm little baby all of her own.

Or perhaps she thought to herself, "When *I'm* a mother, I will still maintain my good looks. I will never let myself go like that poor woman obviously has. How hard can it be, anyway?"

Well, to her, and any other professionally-groomed career women contemplating *my* job, I'd like to say, "You're *so* right! Being an at-home mom is a piece of cake! So, go ahead and pop out a few babies. Watch your last pedicure chip away before your eyes. See your personal time dwindle to a few scattered moments. Observe your hairdo morph from elegant to make-shift. Take notice as your wardrobe accumulates stains from milk and drool and snot. Then come on over to my place, honey. I have an extra pair of slippers, a fresh pot of coffee, and a large bag of potato chips. What are you waiting for?"

A PROMISE

"Do not let your adornment be merely outward—arranging the hair, wearing gold, or putting on fine apparel—rather let it be the hidden person of the heart, with the incorruptible beauty of a gentle and quiet spirit, which is very precious in the sight of God" (1 Peter 3:3-4).

A PRAYER

Lord, forgive my bad attitude about my appearance. I know it's not good for me to make comparisons or to envy other women for being able to put themselves together better than I can. Please help me to do my best to look my best while remembering that You care more about "the hidden person of the heart."

Celeste

"Whenever it rains like this, it reminds me of you," Celeste said to me one day recently, referring to the sudden, short-lived surge of rain in an otherwise clear sky. I smile, knowing just what she means, as I remember...

Shortly after we moved into our new house, we were stopped on the way home from our evening walk by a friendly couple driving through the neighborhood. The man behind the steering wheel asked a boring question about flood insurance companies which Adel promptly answered, leaving us open to more interesting topics such as introductions and ages of children.

Celeste and Tony's eleven month old, Connor, was asleep in his car seat as we talked. I told them we were expecting another baby, pointing to the small mound of my belly that we would later know to be Abby. The conversation ended like any other "meet the neighbors" conversation and we both went our own ways.

A few weeks later, on another walk around the block, we bumped into our new neighbors again. They had recently moved in about ten houses down from us. We approached and picked up the conversation where it left off last time. I noticed right away how comfortable I was talking to Celeste. She listens, asks thoughtful questions, and isn't afraid to make me a part of her life. I feel quite at home in her presence and very free to be myself.

Adel feels equally at ease in Tony's presence, although for completely different reasons. Tony is hardworking, great with children, and surprisingly soft-hearted. He is also sarcastic and seems to thrive on banter, especially when one is foolish enough to engage him in this type of conversation (that would be me). Adel enjoys being around other guys who help him give me a hard time (thanks Tony).

So Celeste and her family became our first friends in our new neighborhood. We shared meals and played cards and dominos, which was great fun. Although I must say, Tony is fiercely competitive, spending the evening verbally pummeling anyone who makes an easy target (which if I open my mouth is, once again, usually me). Connor and Isaac enjoy their time together screaming, throwing things, and running around like banshees.

Early in our friendship, I unintentionally gave Celeste a wonderful opportunity to prove her character. Eight months pregnant with Abby, I was still enjoying my morning exercise walks with Isaac in the stroller and both dogs leashed beside me. On this particular morning I had reached the point on my route that was farthest from home when, from out of the blue, it started to rain. It was like the little black rain cloud that follows a cartoon character around to dampen his spirits. I pulled the stroller cover down over Isaac's head, and with no shelter in sight, I started jogging *gently* toward home (eight months pregnant, remember?). Now this rain was not what I was used to by sunny Southern California standards. This was fierce Texas rain, hard and thick, and stopping as suddenly as it begins.

This particular rainfall had stopped by the time I got back to my driveway, but in that amount of time I was thoroughly soaked. Relieved to be home, I pushed the button on the garage door opener and was dismayed to find, after several subsequent attempts, that the garage door would not budge. The opener was too waterlogged.

I tried to open the garage door manually, but of course it was locked. I walked around to the back door and naturally it was locked as well. Did I have a key? No, dear reader, I did not think to bring a key with me. I was in the habit of going through the garage door and bringing only the garage opener with me on my walks. It never occurred to me that I would be caught in a crazy Texas monsoon that would soak my garage door opener beyond repair.

For a few moments, I stood by my front door, trying not to appear as helpless as I was to the building crew and contractors that were eying me from across the street. I realized that if I had thought to bring along my cell phone, I could have called my husband for help. Naturally, being the dolt that I am, this too never occurred to me.

Since waiting on the porch for eight hours with a toddler isn't really an option, as far as I could tell, I had only two options left:

1. Approach the gawking workmen across the street and ask them to help me break into my own home or

2. Ring the doorbell of my new friend Celeste.

"She's going to think I'm such a dork!" I thought to myself as I walked down the street, half laughing to myself, half willing myself not to make the situation worse by crying about it.

I rang her doorbell, soaking wet, with two dripping dogs, a sopping stroller, and a (thankfully) patient and half wet child (his top half was covered by the stroller canopy but his legs and pants were drenched). Celeste opened the door with a look of surprise. She laughed gently when I told her my situation and welcomed my whole waterlogged crew into her home. I quickly ushered the dogs into the backyard while she brought out dry clothes for Isaac and me.

Then we began to brainstorm my next step. Celeste suggested I stay the day at her place, offering her pack-n-play for Isaac's naptime. Tony, who had the day off, walked back down to my house to see if he would have better luck with my soggy garage door opener. After he returned with no good news, I borrowed a phone book to call Adel. I know, dear reader, I don't believe it either that I can't

69

remember my own husband's cell phone or work number. (Truth be told, even now I don't know his phone numbers by heart. Some people never learn.) Within half an hour Adel arrived, my cavalry in his white motorcycle jacket and helmet, mildly amused and annoyed at the same time.

As for Celeste, when a new friend rings your bell, eight months pregnant, soaked to the bone, helpless, with one tiny child, and two smelly dogs, it would be understandable to cross that friend out of your date book on account of said friend requiring a bit too much effort. But Celeste did nothing of the sort. On the contrary, she proved herself steadfast over the long months ahead as I gave birth and transitioned through the overwhelming adjustment of having *two* young children. It was Celeste who found the mommy group we now both enjoy and who was the first one I would call when I needed a friend. It was a huge blessing to have a friend in my new home who would notice if I suddenly fell off the face of the earth.

A PROMISE

"A man who has friends must himself be friendly, but there is a friend who sticks closer than a brother" (Proverbs 18:24).

A PRAYER

Thank You Lord for providing friends who make me feel at home in their presence and who become like family through the days of our lives. You did not intend for us to go through life alone, and I praise You for the way You consider and provide for our need for companionship.

Simple Tasks

Learning to accomplish small tasks with a new baby is what motherhood is all about. Then that baby becomes a toddler, another new baby joins the crew, and the learning process starts all over again. As for the difficulty of adjusting is concerned, truly the whole is greater than the sum of its parts. The effort of caring for two children is much more than double the effort of caring for one child. At first, every outing with both kids is a trial of ingenuity. How does one run a simple errand with a baby and a toddler? The only way to learn is by doing.

Take this morning for example. Abby is now three months old, sweet and easy-going, and falling into a routine. Isaac is still waking up regularly before the clock strikes six and the sun comes up, leaving him even more grouchy than usual. And my dogs smell.

I have two very fru-fru dogs named Bitsy and Molly. On this particular morning, I have made an appointment for the dogs to get groomed, which I do a few times a year because they smell. I woke up with Isaac at 5:45 AM, tried desperately to sleep a little more as he "snuggled" with me (actually, he used me as a human jungle gym, making sleep impossible for both of us). Then I ate breakfast, fed

Isaac breakfast, showered, gave Isaac a bath, got dressed, dressed Isaac, packed up the car, woke Abby up to nurse at 8:30 AM, dressed Abby, and was at the groomers by 9:00 AM (yay me!).

A simple task like dropping the dogs off at the groomers is no longer simple when you are accompanied by two small children. After pulling into my parking space, I haul the stroller out of the hatchback. Bitsy is yapping away in the front seat as I load Abby into the stroller and then prop Isaac onto the handlebars (after all, this is not a double stroller). I fetch the dogs from the car and we all walk inside the store. We spend three minutes dropping off the dogs and then I return to the car with Isaac and Abby to plunk them down into their car seats once more, and reload the stroller into the hatchback. That's a lot of hauling and hefting for a three minute errand!

After the groomers, we hop over to the next parking lot where I need to run in to get a few things at Target. Again, we unload and reload. It is a nearly uneventful shopping trip (this time) marked only by a diaper blowout by Abby which causes an emergency bathroom stop, and some minor snack bribery on my part to keep Isaac on his bottom in the shopping cart. Twenty minutes later we're back in the car, buckled in and driving across the street to the mall to have lunch, nurse Abby, and let Isaac play as we wait out the rest of our time until we can pick up the dogs.

After the mall, we reload the car and cross back over the street to the groomers. Once there, it appears that Bitsy's haircut is still in the works and they need more time. Okay, we'll just check out the pets in the rest of the store while we wait.

Finally, half an hour later, after we've laughed over a mouse running idiotically in its stationary wheel and a store employee trying to catch a fish that jumps out of the net and onto the floor, I decide we have waited long enough and we head back over to the grooming area to get the dogs, whether they're ready or not. Five minutes later we're all back in the car. The dogs are overly hyper after their morning of captivity. They both have little bows over their ears and smell so much better.

As soon as I begin to buckle Abby into her car seat, she starts to cry. She's hungry again and also ready for her long afternoon nap. Isaac is very tired from his early and active morning and is asleep before I'm on the freeway back home. Abby cries off and on the whole twenty minute drive home. She has just closed her eyes to sleep as I pull in the garage.

I know the next few minutes are going to be unpleasant. Everyone has needs and they all need to be met *right now*! I hop out of the car, carrying my diaper bag and my one bag of purchases from Target. The dogs follow me in the door as I drop the bags on the floor and return quickly to get Abby. With the air conditioning off now, the car is already feeling warm again, even in the garage. Since Abby really hadn't fallen asleep yet, she now has her eyes open. I unbuckle her and carry her inside. She still has tear stains on her cheeks from crying on the way home. As I lay her down on the couch I tell her I'm sorry I can't feed her right away. I have to go get her brother from the car before he melts. She, of course, doesn't understand and starts crying immediately.

With Abby wailing in the background, I return to the hot garage to peel a sweaty Isaac out of his car seat. He remains asleep, slumped over my shoulder, and I carry him past his crying sister to his bedroom upstairs. After plunking him down in his crib, I return downstairs to comfort Abby.

Abby is *angry*. I pick her up and speak soothingly to her as I change her diaper and then sit down to nurse her. She eats like she's starving, eyes rolling back in their lids, even though she nursed only two hours before when we were at the mall. I allow her to suckle for a few minutes after she eats and she is fast asleep before long. I carefully set her in her baby swing and sigh in relief.

Both kids are sleeping! I have a few moments of quiet before Isaac wakes up. Time for dessert! (These days, I always help myself to dessert whenever I get the chance. The way I see it is that the sweets are a little reward to myself after a long morning.) I pour myself a bowl of mini marshmallows and M&Ms and then sneak off to my room to write this entry while both kids remain asleep.

By the time I sit down on my bed and turn on the computer, it's just 12:30 in the afternoon. I feel pretty pleased with this morning's happenings. Already today I have been on the go for almost seven hours. So far I have loaded the kids in and out of the car ten times. I have nursed three times and changed six diapers. I ran two errands and spent quality time with my son. Just a normal morning for a mother with two small children.

A PROMISE

"But you, be strong and do not let your hands be weak, for your work shall be rewarded" (2 Chronicles 15:7).

A PRAYER

Lord, I thank You for a successful day of busy hard work. Thank You for giving me the strength to meet the needs of my children. I know my reward is watching them grow strong and healthy and beautiful.

Learning to Share

With Celeste's inspiration and help, I have now begun to attend some mommy group events with both my kids. Recently we were enjoying a playdate at another mommy's house. At one point Isaac discovered a toy fishing pole that could magnetically catch three or four colorful fish. He thought up a grand procedure wherein he would catch a fish and then pretend to grill it up on the toy barbeque set. He would flip the fish with the turner, sprinkle it with salt, and then pretend to eat it. He played this way for some time, catching and cooking in turn each fish that lay at his feet. Cute, right? Yeah well, it was until he was called upon to share the fish.

Trotting in and out of the playroom, picking up and putting down toys that caught their interest for a few moments, the other children occasionally took interest in the fish. When a child would innocently pick up a fish, it would illicit a howl of fury from Isaac. In Isaac's mind, those fish were *his*. Although he wasn't holding them in his hands at all times, to him they were clearly still part of his game of pretend. And sharing was not a skill that Isaac was learning gracefully.

With each innocent interruption to Isaac's game, I would have to step in to protect the rights of the other children and calm down my irate and imaginative son. On one hand, I felt extremely proud at his complexity of play and I understood his frustration at having his game interrupted. On the other hand, I adhere to the general playtime rule that a toy on the ground is anyone's toy.

At another playdate, his unwillingness to share actually prompted the immergence of his inner-bully. Isaac was sporting his first buzz cut, the result of Mommy's carelessness with the electric shaver. He was looking every bit the "tough guy" with his new crew cut. His summer tan added to the effect, making him look like one of those street kids of the 1950's who would spend his time throwing rocks at stray dogs and kicking holes in the neighbors' nice picket fences. Well, on this particular day, Isaac lived up to this image.

I feel quite certain we can blame Isaac's violent day on the early introduction his *father* gave him to the world of video games. Isn't it always safe to blame all child-related violence on video games? Then there are the hours Isaac has spent at home wrestling with his *father* and trying gallantly to knock him unconscious with his plastic light saber. Is it equally safe to blame *fathers* for child-related violence? Probably not, but anything to make *me* feel better, right?

At this particular playdate, as I was loading a plate of goodies from the snack bar, I turned at the sound of unfamiliar crying. Isaac was standing suspiciously close to the upset child, so I asked the child's mother if Isaac did something. "Oh, he just hit her and took the toy," the mother replied, kindly trying to make it sound as if my child were not the untamed, savage beast that he was beginning to appear.

Isaac was sent to time-out. A few minutes went by, we talked, we hugged, and I released him with hope back into the community of happy children. Then I foolishly attempted to start up a trivial conversation with another mommy, catching another random act of joyful violence from Isaac out of the corner of my eye. In the time it took me to cross the room to apprehend the offender, he had gleefully attacked two other children, bombing them with toys from across the room. His aim was deadly accurate.

In my mind's eye, children were strewn about the room wearing little X's on their eyes to show they had become victims of the bully, Isaac standing in the middle laughing wickedly. In reality, the children hardly noticed they'd been attacked and the other mothers were extremely sympathetic to my efforts. There was another time-out, this one longer, followed by a talk and a warning about leaving at the next offense no matter how slight. We concluded with another hug and a face-to-face apology to his victims.

Moments later, he was at it again, this time pushing down the two remaining kids who had managed to escape his first and second attacks. I made my embarrassed apologies to the mommies and hauled Isaac out the door, while Abby slumped helplessly over my arm, going with the flow as usual. Naturally, I lectured all the way home about how he wasn't going to have any friends if he kept hurting people. Naturally, he didn't hear a word I said as he was busy trying to use his toes to pull the cord out of the car DVD player.

Another day, during a weekend at my mom's house, we were all enjoying a noisy afternoon family gathering. My sister and her husband and two little girls were there too, so with four kids under the age of three it was pretty rambunctious. Isaac, notoriously possessive of his toys, was living up to his reputation by hitting his girl cousins on the head for so much as thinking about taking his toy. In this case, the toy in question was a shiny new harmonica that he had received from his Mimi.

At one point, his cousin Lily approached and looked covetously at his harmonica, to which he responded by bopping her on the head. I was not in the room at the time so my sister appropriately escorted Isaac to time-out. Then she returned to the kitchen where the rest of us were working on dinner.

As she approached, she had a suppressed giggle on her face. We all looked up to find out why she was laughing, and she pointed around the corner to where Isaac was sitting. When she had escorted him to time-out, she had forgotten to take away the offending harmonica. The result was a harmonious interchange of nasal whining and metallic wheezing. Here's how it went:

(Child Whining) "Mommy!"
(Harmonica Wheezing) W*rrreeeeeWrrrrrrrrWrrreeeeeWrrrrrrrr*
(Child Whining) "Mommy, I want to get out!"
(Harmonica Wheezing) W*rrreeeeeWrrrrrrrrWrrreeeeeWrrrrrrrr*
(Child Whining) "Waaaaa…"
(Harmonica Wheezing) W*rrreeeeeeeeWrrrrrrrrrrrWrrreeeeeeee*
(Child Whining) "Mommy, I want to get out now!"
(Harmonica Wheezing) W*rrreeeeeWrrrrrrrrWrrreeeeeWrrrrrrrr*

At this point our stifled giggles were drawing tears and our faces were turning red from the effort of not laughing out loud.
(Child Whining) "Mommy…"
(Harmonica Wheezing) W*rrreeeeeWrrrrrrrrWrrreeeeeWrrrrrrrr*
(Child Whining) "Waaaaa…"
(Harmonica Wheezing) W*rrreeeeeWrrrrrrrrWrrreeeeeWrrrrrrrr*
(Child Whining) "Mommy! I want to get out now!"
(Harmonica Wheezing) W*rrreeeeeeeeWrrrrrrrrrrrWrrreeeeeeee*

We let it go on for much longer than a normal time-out simply because it was such a good laugh. I think even Isaac was having a good time. The harmonica oversight had entertained us with the most melodious rendition of "The Time-Out Blues." It was truly a performance we'll never forget. I'm not sure he learned his lesson about sharing though.

Isaac has made some progress along this road. He applies the concept of trading one toy for another. When another (usually smaller) child has something he wants (say, a battery-powered, remote-control race car with flashing lights and cool sound effects) he will pick up the nearest toy (say, a single, discarded, red block) and hand it to the other child while he nabs the toy he wants out of the younger child's hand. The other child will stand there, looking down at the block thinking, "Seriously, what am I supposed to do with this block?"

Okay, he still has some learning to do in this area. We'll get there, I hope. At least by the time he's twenty!

A PROMISE

"But the fruit of the Spirit is love, joy, peace, longsuffering, kindness, goodness, faithfulness, gentleness, self-control. Against such there is no law" (Galatians 5:22-23).

A PRAYER

Lord please help me teach my child the fruit of gentleness. Give me the patience to be consistent with my instructing and redirecting so that he will eventually learn to solve his problems without anger and violence. Thank You for his fiery spirit, so much like my own at times. I praise You that, just as I love my child in spite of his waywardness, so You also love me in spite of my own.

If Only

Anyone who has been a parent for more than a millisecond knows this fundamental rule of parenting: *never* go out in public with a child who is too tired or too hungry. Most parents would rather stick their head inside the mouth of a crocodile than attempt public negotiations with a tired, hungry toddler. Unfortunately for me, avoiding this situation is not always possible and it makes for some unpleasant situations.

As I have previously mentioned, Isaac has not been sleeping well lately. Let's just say he fervently believes that avoiding sleep is one of his inalienable rights. This leaves him more than a bit on the grumpy side. However, he still has more energy than a barrel of monkeys on speed (who all have ants in their pants) and so life must go on. Thus, in spite of his general funk, I dared to take Isaac to our favorite indoor play area today.

At the play area, Abby watched from her usual position at the crook of my arm while Isaac made his way around the room. I hate lugging the car seat around so Abby often finds her little self in the crook of my arm. I do own about three different types of slings and carriers but sometimes it just doesn't seem worth it to untangle the contraptions and use them. Especially when I am with my new mommy friends—then there's always an extra pair of arms if I'm in a crunch. "Can you hold Abby for a sec?" Unfortunately, although the room was filled with people, this day we traveled alone. Looking back, this was one of those times that hauling the sling or carrier would have been so very much worth the effort.

As the time neared for us to go home, I gave Isaac the five-minute warning, the two-minute warning, and the one-minute warning. Then I gave him the, "You can go down the slide *one more time* and then we'll go put on your shoes" warning. Just for the record, I want to clarify that I did all of this *by the book*. I am certainly not a perfect parent, but I'm *trying* here. You get points for effort, right?

Anyway, just as I issued the last warning and Isaac took his last slide down, things got really ugly. Isaac, asserting his iron will, did not want to go put on his shoes. When I grabbed his hand to guide him in the right direction, his legs crumpled and he melted in a whining heap on the floor. I bent down, Abby's head bobbing, in an attempt to speak to him at his eye level (kind of impossible with a kid who is horizontal but I was trying to do things *by the book!*). I repeated several times, in several different tones, the need for us to go home. He remained prostrate.

Feeling myself out of options and already embarrassed by our public display of pandemonium, I searched for a quick way to end the confrontation. I leaned my head as close to his as possible and through gritted teeth (not so much *by the book*) I threatened a spanking if he did not comply. He remained prostrate.

If the world could have frozen in that instant, I would have had the time to take a step back and see the situation clearly:

Here is a small child asserting his will-power over his mother. He's irrational from being hungry and tired and two years old. He has had <u>enough</u> of sharing his mommy with his strange, new, baby sister *and he's determined to get his mom's attention one way or another.*

Here is a mother who was at her wit's end with this child before the day even began because of the on-going struggle over sleep. She is distracted and physically divided by the fact that she has to hold her infant in her arms while dealing with her toddler (oh how she wishes for that car seat or baby sling now!). Her agitation is made worse by her perception of cold glances of the other mothers in the room (or is it just her imagination?).

Here is a situation that will end without a winner. Everyone loses.

I felt the eyes of nearby mothers on me and I burned with embarrassment at not being able to control my two year old. I know what they must have been thinking. Half of them, probably those with younger children who have never had a temper tantrum before, would have been thinking, "I will never be *that* kind of mother." I know they were thinking this because I have thought it myself when watching other mothers discipline their children. This thought is a necessary impulse for every new mother, almost as automatic as breathing. The other half, those who have been down this road before, would have been thinking, "Poor fool. How embarrassing for her. Glad it's not *me* this time!" At that moment I wished for the superpower to evaporate myself along with my two children and have us magically appear in the privacy of our own home. I wanted to escape the unsympathetic audience to my inadequacy.

Having made the threat of a spanking, and really seeing no other alternative, I used my one free arm to yank him to his feet. Isaac chose this moment to demonstrate that he is quite an accomplished knee-buckler. His knee-buckling efforts forced me to yank him up from the floor repeatedly, causing Abby's infant head to bobble up and down on my arm as often as I jerked him up. The three of us were creating quite a scene and I was pretty sure I would melt from embarrassment at any moment. When I finally had him standing for more than a split second, I gave him a swift, impotent pat on the rear. The swat probably was barely enough to be felt through his diaper but it kept him on his feet long enough for me to drag him over to our bag. I pinned my unprotesting Abby between my legs while I wrestled Isaac into his shoes. The whole time, he was kicking and shouting "I DON'T WANT TO!" Threatening a more serious spank than the wimpy one he had just received, I dragged him (resisting and whining all the way) out the door.

Oh, how I wish I could say it all ended there at the door. Unfortunately, the downward spiral continued. Once outside, his knees crumpled again. This time we were removed a bit from our audience, although if they had really been trying to follow our gripping saga, they could have easily seen us through the windows. I hauled him over my knee (with one arm since I was still holding Abby) and spanked him a bit harder. This spank was still not hard enough to really hurt but it at least registered a sound. He began to really cry, melting into a sorrowful heap on my lap. I saw that, for a moment at least, he was defeated. Trying for a connection during this brief moment of surrender, I gave him a hug, told him I would put Abby in her car seat, and then talk to him some more.

We were right next to the car and he stood there on the sidewalk crying while I buckled Abby in. After she was secure, I picked him up (glad to finally have two hands) and talked to him soothingly: "I'm sorry I had to spank you, Isaac, but you need to obey Mommy. When Mommy says it's time to go, you need to go. I love you." He was slightly consoled, less by my words than by my undivided attention.

Unfortunately, undivided attention is a scarce commodity in our house these days. The moment had to end and we had to drive

83

home. He freaked out again when I put him in his car seat. And he screamed the whole way home.

Once home, I was able to give him a few more minutes of undivided attention since Abby had fallen asleep. I fed him lunch and put him down for his nap. What would I change if I could go back? I would bring the car seat for Abby! If only, if only I could have swept up Isaac's prostrate, protesting body in my arms and held him gently but firmly until he stopped his battle. If only, if only I could have used *both hands* to hold him up so I could speak softly eye to eye with him and try to sooth his madness. If only, if only I had what it takes, *all the time*, to be the mother I so wish I could be.

A PROMISE

"So I said, 'Oh, that I had wings like a dove! I would fly away and be at rest. Indeed, I would wander far off, and remain in the wilderness. I would hasten my escape from the windy storm and tempest...As for me, I will call upon God, and the Lord shall save me. Evening and morning and at noon I will pray, and cry aloud, and He shall hear my voice...Cast your burden on the Lord, and He shall sustain you; He shall never permit the righteous to be moved" (Psalm 55, verses 6-8, 16-17, 22).

A PRAYER

Oh, that I had a neck like an ostrich! I would hide my head in a hole in the ground and be at rest. Lord, I often find myself incapable of parenting with gracefulness. My integrity and emotions fail me when I need them most of all. God, help me to respond only as You would to the misbehaviors of my children. I ask You to sustain me when my heart is overwhelmed with my own inadequacies. Be my constant companion in this monumental task of raising my children.

Personal Grooming

When I decided to have kids it never occurred to me that the challenge of personal grooming would grow exponentially with each new child I added to my family. Now that I have two kids, personal grooming is actually *twenty* times as difficult. One face to wash becomes three. So you might assume that it would be merely *three* times as difficult. However, if you multiply that by ninety distractions per minute, you will get exponential growth of the "difficulty factor." Twenty nails to cut become sixty but add to that chore eighteen failed attempts to cut *one* nail on a wiggling toddler and you see how I mean "exponentially" more difficult.

This thinking is a little mathematical for a "creative-type" person like me. In fact, some of the numbers and calculations I'm dealing with would make for a good SAT question:

> *A young mother has twenty-eight teeth. Her two-year-old son has twenty teeth and her four-month-old daughter has no teeth yet but will start growing teeth any day now. The mother wants to brush everyone's teeth twice a day as the dentist recommends. There is a*

strong wind blowing in from the northwest and sweater
season is almost upon them. How many teeth should she
be brushing each day?

My calculations look something like this:

(28 teeth + 20 teeth + X amount of teeth) multiplied by brushing 2 times a day, multiplied again by the exponential difficulty factor = dental hygiene responsibilities up the wazoo!

Brushing my own teeth always takes preeminence over my children's. After all, the new friends *they're* meeting at our play dates care more about what toy they're playing with than whether or not their breath smells minty fresh. However, I'm pretty sure *my* new friends are quite happy that I find the time to brush my teeth each day. Most days Isaac and I wrestle over the battery-powered fire-truck toothbrush, accomplishing more havoc-creating than actual brushing of teeth. Abby is lucky if I just show her a toothbrush every now and then.

While there are some areas of personal grooming that I won't compromise, my deodorant for example, other areas, like nail clipping, get put off far past their time. Generally I don't notice my kids nails need to be trimmed until one of two things occurs:

1. Isaac has black guck under his nails or

2. Abby scratches very close to my eye with her "Freddy Kruger death nails" as she tries to lovingly investigate my various facial orifices.

I simply can't keep up. This leads me to ponder what I would do if the number of nails I had to cut went up from sixty to eighty or even a hundred or more? With the third child, I would probably start to encourage nail biting. With the fourth and subsequent children, I'd probably go all out with the hopes of landing my family a spot in *The Guinness Book of World Records* for "family with the longest fingernails." Does that come with a cash reward? Because that would be pretty cool!

Then there's ear wax. Nobody told me that I was supposed to regularly clean out my kids' ears. In fact, doctors have led me to believe otherwise, scaring me away from using Q-tips by citing the many cases of Q-tip-induced ear infections and ear drum ruptures. So, at the age of two, Isaac's wax build up resembled something from a low-budget rendition of "Return of the Attack of the Avenging Swamp Booger." So now, every once in a while, I get a wet washcloth and dab around in there with the hope of curbing another return/attack/revenge. Who knew?

Lastly, let's talk about laundry. I now wash ginormous amounts of bedding, towels, and clothing on a weekly basis. It's another one of those never-ending chores. Sometimes I'm tempted to strip my kids down right in front of the washing machine and let them run around naked just so I can have ONE DAY where all our clothes are clean at the same time! Wouldn't that be great?! And my kids are not even the size of real humans yet. They're more like the size of large poultry. What's going to happen to our laundry loads when they are both teenagers, wearing 3.5 pairs of jeans *every day*?

We will be doing eighteen loads of laundry every week. Aaaaaah!

Okay, Megan, calm down. You have to realize that by then your kids will be able to wash their own laundry.

Thanks, Megan. That does make me feel better. But what about the water and energy bills with so many loads?

You can teach your kids the value of conservation by re-wearing clothes that are clearly not smelly or dirty.

I see.

You could also teach them responsibility by having them help pay for the bills with their allowance or, heaven forbid, actually getting a job and contributing to the household's financial well-being. Or you could limit the amount of laundry they wash to what they can accomplish out back with a basin, a washboard, and a bar of soap.

Those ideas are pretty far-fetched, but what worries me even more is that I seem to be having a conversation with myself. Should I be worried about this?

No. It is perfectly normal, especially for overworked stay-at-home mothers who are prone to hallucinations.

Great, thanks!

A PROMISE
"Take My yoke upon you and learn from Me, for I am gentle and lowly in heart, and you will find rest for your souls. For My yoke is easy and My burden is light" (Matthew 11:29-30).

A PRAYER
Lord, even little things like teeth and nails seem to add up against me these days. Constantly feeling overwhelmed and overrun leaves me worn out and weary. I love that You promise me rest for my soul. Right now I would settle for rest for my body or really any kind of rest at all, but rest for my soul sounds particularly heavenly. I praise You for knowing me and loving me so well that You know and care when I am weary and You offer me rest in Your arms.

Mission Control

A PERSPECTIVE

Every now and then a Cheerio comes flying out of the air vent of my car. You may be wondering how this happened. But more likely, if you've ever occupied the same hemisphere as a toddler, how it happened might be all too obvious.

We often allow Isaac to climb into the car and play while we're loading or unloading it. He loves to pretend to drive and explore the fascinating "mommy-and-daddy-only" area. He will start in the driver's seat, handling all of the knobs, pushing all the buttons, and tweaking anything tweakable. Then he'll move to the second row, testing out the car seats before climbing into the hatchback section to pretend he's in a spaceship or camping tent or whatever.

Mimi emailed me a great description of one of Isaac's imaginary car escapades. She entitled it "Commander Isaac":

> Boppa drives his Highlander with all aboard into the Lagoy driveway and cuts the engine. Mimi and Boppa get out and assist Megan in releasing Abby from her car seat in the tiny third row. All are now out of the car but Isaac, who, on the

instant of being unsnapped from his car seat harness by Adel, scrambles to the front and into the driver's seat. Megan laughs and tells us he always does this after a trip. He's playing 'mission control.'

Apparently, Isaac must defend our ship from attacking aliens, because he wastes no time in blasting off into orbit. "Five, four, three, two, one, blastoff!" he shouts in his commander voice as he purposefully pushes buttons, clicks clickers, and switches switches.

Boppa, watching from the bridge (with a lack of imagination) says, "Hey, turn off the hazard lights."

Isaac, in full control, shouts, "No, I need them!"

Now Boppa understands the importance of this mission, and when Isaac turns on the cruise control, he says, "I see you turned on the thrusters. Good idea." Isaac doesn't seem to notice as he steers frantically and keeps all the instruments on the panel under his careful and active control, all to the sounds of intense ray-gun fire (provided by himself).

After this sustained battle, Boppa says, "You've gained orbit now, so you can turn off your thrusters" and to his surprise, Isaac immediately turns off the cruise control. This kid knows his thrusters.

And the harshness of battle just rolls off his back. The mission is suddenly over and the commander scrambles into the house to work on his Lego train.

Almost every time we allow this type of activity, there are certain "adjustments" we can expect to make upon our next trip in the car. Before backing out of the driveway, we must run through a simple checklist:

- Turn off headlights
- Turn off high beams
- Reopen air vents
- Close all compartments
- Turn off windshield wipers
- Turn off turn signal
- Close window on hatchback
- Readjust rearview mirror

It seems like a lot of extra work when you're accustomed to simply snapping your seatbelt shut and turning on the engine, but you get used to it.

However, Isaac's latest car exploration adventure has resulted in my most unusual and unfortunate discovery of Cheerios crammed into the air vents. "What to do?" thought I, as I readjusted the rearview mirror. "I have never seen the likes of this before." I recalled the several objects in irretrievable locations we have strewn throughout our home: a marker down the shower drain; a toy rocket in the fireplace key-hole; a bead necklace in the bathtub drain. And those are just the ones I know about. But having the air vents of the car stuffed with Cheerios? Surely, this can be fixed?

So, I turned on the air. Nothing happened at first. But then, a few adjustments, an increase in airflow, a wiggle of my finger, and Cheerios came spraying out, machine-gun style. That's one vent down and three to go. I called for Bitsy (the dog) to jump in the car and "clean up" the mess. Then I grabbed my things and went inside the house.

I figured the rest could wait. After all, I knew that inside I was probably awaited by more urgent issues than Cheerios in the air vents. I had left Abby on the floor in her car seat, vulnerable to big-brother attack. And Isaac had been inside for a few minutes already and was probably trying to cram a giant stuffed animal into the toilet. Thus I decided to leave the rest of the vents as temporary holding bays for Isaac's arsenal of cereal. I knew they'd come out eventually. So now, every once in a while as I'm driving, a wayward Cheerio flies out of nowhere. I smile and remember.

A PROMISE

"Rejoice always, pray without ceasing, in everything give thanks; for this is the will of God in Christ Jesus for you" (1 Thessalonians 5:16-18).

A PRAYER

Lord, I rejoice in the creativity, imagination, and energy You have given to my child. Thank You for making him so unique and special. I'm grateful that You grant me a spirit of peace about the little things. When I'm willing to accept Your peace, I can truly enjoy the adventures of my child!

Devotional

I've started reading a devotional for toddlers as part of Isaac's bedtime routine. It has a daily story or scenario with pictures, a bible verse, and a rhyming prayer. He is *just* mature enough to follow along as I read (sometimes).

One night the devotional was about God's power and strength. On the page was a landscape picture of a countryside with some houses and sheep in the distance. It described how powerful a king or ruler is and then said that God is more powerful than any king.

Since Isaac was being silly and squirmy during the brief reading, I felt the need to drill the point home with some follow up questions. Here's how it went:

Mommy: God is so powerful. He's stronger than a king! Do you want to be a king?

Isaac: I want to be a giant!

Mommy: Okay. Did you know God is stronger than a giant?

Isaac: (*doubtful*) Noooo?

Mommy: God is stronger than **everybody**. (*testing*) Is a **king** stronger than God?

Isaac: Noooo?

Mommy: Right! Is a **giant** stronger than God?

Isaac: Noooo.

Mommy: Is **Mommy** stronger than God?

Isaac: (*laughing*) Noooo!

Mommy: Is **Daddy** stronger than God?

Isaac: (*with growing enthusiasm*) No!!

Mommy: (*trying to think of the biggest person in our family for extra emphasis*) What about Boppa? Is **Boppa** stronger than God?

Isaac: (*yelling with confidence*) NO!!

Mommy: (*feeling satisfaction that he gets the point*) Right! No one is stronger than God!

Isaac: (*scheming*) Say Mimi!

Mommy: You want me to ask you if Mimi's stronger than God?

Isaac: (*excited*) Yes! Say Mimi!

Mommy: Okay. Is **Mimi** stronger than God?

Isaac: (*pauses, then yells as if getting to the punch line*) YES!!!

Naturally I felt the need to tickle him for this response, after which followed a short game of naming names, yelling "no" and "yes" repeatedly, and lots of tickling. Interestingly, Isaac's candid response shows he knows who really calls the shots around here!

Another night, another children's devotional.

This time the lesson was "God is everywhere." After reading, Isaac got "that look" in his eyes that revealed he was *really* thinking about it. I can always tell "that look" because he will gaze slightly up and to the side, as if there's a picture in his mind's eye that he's studying. When he has this look, you can almost hear the gears spinning in his imaginative brain.

And when he gets excited about an idea, he loves to act it out. He slowly stood up, a big grin on his face. Then he started walking in big steps around the room with his arms spread, glancing slowly from side to side.

Mommy: Isaac, what are you doing?

Isaac: I'm going to find God!

Mommy: Well, we can't *see* God, but He's everywhere. He lives in You and in Me and everywhere in our house.

Isaac: (*pauses to consider this; then begins running with heavy, stomping footprints, a sly glimmer in his eye*)

Mommy: Now what are you doing?

Isaac: I'm going to step on Him!

A PROMISE

"One generation shall praise Your works to another, and shall declare Your mighty acts" (Psalm 145:4).

A PRAYER

Father, it is so important to me to teach my children about Your mighty acts. I want them to know the wonderful stories of the Bible as well as the mighty acts You have done in my own life. Please help me to be diligent to read and talk with them about You and to teach them to talk with You in prayer. I pray that as they grow they will choose on their own to follow You and love You the way I do.

Redefining a Good Day

A PERSPECTIVE

Abby's now five months old and I've become fairly competent at caring for both of my children. Although tired, by the evening I have the warm, happy satisfaction of knowing that Isaac had fun each day and Abby had her simple needs met in a timely manner. I take pride in my newly learned multitasking skills and in the fact that Adel and I are actually able to exchange a few brief words of interesting conversation when he returns home from work (it's a great improvement over the days when I would frantically meet him at the door with a poopy diaper in hand and the words "help me!" written in crayon across my forehead). In these simple accomplishments, I am learning to take great joy. I'm doing it! I'm learning how to be a mother of two!

However, along with my growing capabilities, there is a murky dissatisfaction lurking in the corners of my mind. It is beginning to irk me that the grand total of my daily accomplishments sums up to providing for the immediate needs of my children, *and nothing more*. Cleaning the house? Fat chance! Projects? Never heard of 'em! Investing time and energy in developing friendships? Maybe next year! Pulling weeds? Ha! My house is a disorganized mess, the greatest project I've accomplished in the past month was plucking my eyebrows, I still have only one actual friend here in Texas who would notice if I fell off the face of the earth, and our weeds are threatening to take over the world! For five months I have put off everything that wasn't necessary for survival, and I'm weary of simply surviving.

I recently decided that I have been wimping out for long enough, using the excuse of being swamped with my kids. Shouldn't I be better at this by now and able to take on new tasks? Surely! So I said to my self, "Self, it's high time you accomplish something!"

With that, I redefined what constitutes a good day:

Old Definition: A good day is one in which all members of the household are relatively content and have their most basic needs met in a timely manner: the mother will get a shower; the child will get his playtime; the baby will be clean and well-nourished; and the father will not have to come home to complete and utter chaos.

New Definition: A good day is one in which all the requirements of the Old Definition are still met. Added to that, the mother must also demonstrate a high degree of *control* over the daily activities of her family. She must run her household with *efficiency, creativity,* and *organization.* She must graduate from surviving within the walls of her own home to making a positive impact on people outside of her household. She must be all things to all people. She must earn the admiration of her peers, the praise of her husband, and the gratitude of her children. She must earn her own respect as well through her various accomplishments. And she must strive, strive, strive until she achieves all of this.

Sounds like a blast, right? Well, believe me; I tried it and it so wasn't! With my new definition in hand, I set some new goals for myself this morning. They were simple goals, like looking up new recipes (I didn't say anything about actually cooking them!) and working on my writing. But, I figured that if I could accomplish these simple tasks, then surely I would be on my way to world domination!

So, while Isaac played at my feet and Abby napped in the swing, I tried to look up recipes. However, I found only one viable recipe and left a mess of cookbooks on the living room couch, many suffering ripped and crumpled pages as a result of Isaac's curiosity. Urg! Frustration! Total Accomplishments = Zero. During Isaac's naptime, my plan was to have a quiet time, check my email, call an acquaintance to invite for dinner, and then work on my writing. Instead, I opened my Bible and said an obligatory and frantic prayer (does that count as quality time with God?). Then I hurriedly opened my laptop to check email and maybe do some writing. But, when Isaac woke up after only half an hour, I felt a great lack of accomplishment and yearned to achieve more.

Soon Abby was awake from her nap too and I was feeling thoroughly overwhelmed and defeated. Total Accomplishments = A Big Fat Zero! The droning message that kept playing in my head was: *Is this it? Am I sentenced heretofore to days upon end of obscurity, impotence, and irrelevance? I want to be somebody. I want to do something! I could accomplish great things if only I could find the time between diaper changes, Candy Land, and nose wipes.*

And I'm a well-spring of great intentions. Stacked on my desk is a pile of pictures and empty frames, waiting for me to arrange and mount proudly on our walls, because that's the kind of homemaker I want to be. In the closet, Adel's brand new pants wait to be hemmed because that's the kind of wife I want to be. On the floor next to my desk, sits a crumpled pile of papers that contain my chicken-scratch drawings for our future homemade sandbox, garage organization system, and covered patio, because that's the kind of homeowner I want to be. Heaped on my kitchen counter, large tasty boxes of candy, popcorn bags, and sodas, wait to be assembled into "date night" gift packages for my new friends who have just had babies, because that's the kind of friend I want to be. All these wishful projects, all these lofty goals, and nothing to show for it except a bad attitude.

I must confess friends, my problem is largely due to the fact that I'm a Martha on steroids. If you're not sure what I'm alluding to, read Luke 10:38-42. There are these two sisters who invite Jesus to come to their house. Martha, the good hostess, spends her time cooking, cleaning, and preparing (you go, girl!). Her sister Mary just sits the whole time at Jesus' feet, listening to his teaching. Naturally Martha gets frustrated and calls upon the Rabbi to correct her lazy sister (preach it, sister!). However, to Martha's surprise, Jesus instead commends Mary for choosing the one thing that is most important (wait...*what?!*).

Is this implying that even in motherhood, I am supposed to be like Mary, content with sitting at the feet of Jesus? Does this mean that, in the midst of mothering two young children, I should not, like Martha, find myself striving, striving, and uselessly striving to do more? In that case, if the only thing I'm able to accomplish in a day is raising my children and spending time in the presence of my Lord, then I should count myself joyfully blessed!

Sure, meeting the combined needs of my kids is like trying to keep a troop of hungry monkeys from stealing my bananas: it takes constant, unceasing effort to keep from being overrun. But it hurts us all when I regard my children's needs as interruptions to my own agenda. Right now, caring for them *is* my agenda. When my Martha alter-ego turns her evil eye upon me, I need to protect myself from useless striving by reminding myself of the great tribute God has given me through the gift of entrusting me with my children. Look at these children! God is allowing me the divine privilege of helping Him to shape them!

And what's more, if I'll let Him, He wants to sit by my side and help me with this monumental task. His desire is to offer me all of Himself so that I, in turn, am filled enough to offer my children all of myself. What more can I ask than this? What an honor! What a joy! What a blessing!

A PROMISE

"And whatever you do in word or deed, do all in the name of the Lord Jesus, giving thanks to God the Father through Him" (Colossians 3:17).

A PRAYER

God, sometimes I get so frustrated that I'm not able to accomplish my own goals because of the overwhelming needs of my children. Help me to remember that *everything* I do, most especially the nurturing of my children, I am supposed to do in Your name. If it is all I can accomplish to glorify You through the way I use my words and deeds in interacting with my children, may that be the sweetest offering to You and the most rewarding accomplishment to my soul.

Dinosaur Show

A PERSPECTIVE

Recently I left Abby with my mom and took Isaac to see a dinosaur show in which life-sized dinosaurs roamed the stage, roaring and trying to eat each other. We went with two other mommies and their little boys. I hoped it would be a good opportunity for me to get to know the other two mothers better and also gain some valuable and rare mother-son time.

The show was an intense spectacle. Learning about dinosaurs is one thing. Having them walking around up-close and personal was an incredible experience. Isaac was by far the most scared of the bunch. He sat like a stone on my lap, fingers in his mouth, not even noticing the snacks I kept offering. I was a bit worried that he'd lose it completely so I tried to talk him through the show as much as I could:

At the beginning of the show, lights come up on a large nest of eggs as the narrating "paleontologist" describes the life of a typical dinosaur. The eggs begin to hatch and little baby dinosaurs wiggle their heads out, controlled from underneath the rock they're sitting on by human puppeteers.

Me: Isaac, do you see the dinosaur eggs?

Isaac: (*silently points, indicating he indeed sees the aforementioned eggs*)

Me: Look, Isaac, the baby dinosaurs are hatching!

Isaac: (*points again, a look of awe crossing his face...from this moment on he has been OBSESSED with baby-any-things hatching out of eggs*)

The narrator goes on describing the life and times of dinosaurs as a rather large dino enters the stage.

Me: Oh wow, Isaac! Look, it's the mommy dinosaur! Isn't she big!?

Isaac: (*presses his back farther into to my ribcage, and nods apprehensively*)

The dinosaur rounds the stage and approaches the eggs, eyeing the hatchlings sideways in a birdlike manner.

Me: Look, Isaac, the mommy dinosaur is going to say "hi" to her babies!

Isaac: (*points again to acknowledge that he is following this plot with rapt attention*)

The large dinosaur then proceeds to pick up one the vulnerable babies in his mouth and chomp down on its limp and helpless body until clearly it is dead.

Me: (*positive I've done irreparable damage to Isaac's psyche*) Or maybe that wasn't the *mommy* dinosaur.

Isaac: (*stares, mouth agape at the scene of horror he has just witnessed*)

Me: No, that wasn't the mommy dinosaur. That was a *bad* dinosaur!

Another, larger dinosaur enters. This one is clearly the mother of the babies as they are actually shaped the same...a detail I failed to hone in on initially.

Me: Look, Isaac! (*my voice still trying for cheerful after that monumental blunder*) Here's the *real* mommy dinosaur! She's coming to protect her babies! Hooray!

Isaac: (*claps his hands automatically and slowly, as if my words are registering in his shocked state, but he is still wide-eyed and he is clearly traumatized*)

The mommy dinosaur, due to her larger bulk is able to waylay the predator and eventually chases it off the stage, but not without much roaring and gnashing of teeth. When the "bad guy" finally gives up and stalks off stage, Isaac exhales for the first time in fifteen minutes and claps his hands with an actual smile on his face.

During intermission, Isaac returns to his normal energetic antics, playing roughly with the two other toddler boys who came with us. They pretend to maul each other with the tiny toy dinosaurs we've brought with us. Isaac hesitates when we tell him it's time to return to our seats. He was probably glad to have made it out alive and has no idea why we would want to willingly go back there where dinosaurs are eating each other for lunch. But peer pressure is a powerful thing and he follows suit, clutching my hand.

He does fine for the remainder of the show, never easing the stunned look from his face, or relaxing the tense ball of arms and legs that he's managed to entangle in my lap. At the very end of the show, a baby t-rex comes out and gets itself cornered by two larger carnivorous dinosaurs. But not to worry, for the grand finale here comes...drum roll please...the mommy t-rex! Isaac again claps automatically but the look on his face indicates he doesn't know whether to cheer or run.

The giant t-rex of course chases the other two aggressors away and then has a heartwarming snuggle with her offspring before bellowing an enormous roar into the stadium across from us. The crowd laughs when the baby t-rex tries out his own lungs in a roar that sounds more like the horn on our Toyota Matrix.

The mommy t-rex then crosses to the front of the arena, bellowing into the faces of the audience members who occupy exactly our level of seating. Our side is next, and we watch in awe as the beast ambles over to us, her giant mouth at eye-level. I think to myself, *this is it. Isaac has been hanging on by a thread this whole time, and when that thing roars in his face, he's going to lose it completely!* Much to my relief, the t-rex decides to leave our side of the auditorium with a dominating glare instead of a roar and we all cheer as she ushers her offspring back offstage.

Isaac remembers the show quite well when we mention it and occasionally acts out parts for us using his toy dinosaur collection. When asked what his favorite part was, he will say when the baby t-rex roared and everyone laughed. If you ask him whether he wants to watch it again he will sometimes say *yes* and sometimes say *no* "because it was too scary." Go ahead and ask him what the scariest part was...he'll tell you it was when the mommy dinosaur ate her baby. See, scarred for life!

105

A PROMISE

"Do not be afraid of sudden terror, nor of trouble from the wicked when it comes; for the Lord will be your confidence and will keep your foot from being caught" (Proverbs 3:25-26).

A PRAYER

Lord, I'm struck by how much fear a child can overcome simply by being nestled in the arms of his loving mother. Just like a loving mother, Your love is enough to conquer even sudden terrors. When I am afraid of noises in the dark or of "what-ifs" too terrible to imagine, I am comforted by knowing that Your loving arms are continually encompassing me and Your still, small voice is soothing my fears.

Comfort Objects

The long months of sleep wars with Isaac seem to be finally coming to an end. We have reached a tolerable truce. Isaac sleeps until a decent hour in the morning and his naps are slowly stretching back out to a more appropriate length of time. The thirty-minute nap is now a deviation from the norm, rather than the standard.

Even our bedtime routine has finally become less stressful. We have been doing the same bedtime routine since he was old enough to sit still and read. After dinner we play as a family. Then we get Isaac ready for bed. We read a few books together, say a prayer, and then Isaac kisses Daddy and Abby goodnight. Mommy stays a few minutes longer to tuck him in and sing him a bedtime song. At first Isaac could not tolerate soft and sweet lullabies. They made him pucker out his lower lip and start to whimper and sniff. So for the longest time his favorite bedtime songs were "Head, Shoulders, Knees, and Toes," "I'm a Policeman Dressed in Blue," and "Casey Junior's Coming Down the Track." Finally, I was able to ease him into some actual lullabies and he now can't live without "Baby Mine."

I have spent so much of the past year just trying to get Isaac to go willingly into his bed that we've sort of created another monster in the process. A trick I learned over the months of bedtime battles was that letting Isaac pick out a special toy to bring to bed with him seems to make the transition go more smoothly. But the monster occurred when the toys began to conglomerate in his crib. And heaven forbid I should ever try to remove one! If I have the finesse to clean out the toy stash on the sly, it is possible for me to have a measure of success. But trying to remove one of the dozens of "precious" and "irreplaceable" objects from his bed *in his presence* is not a task I have yet managed to master.

Don't worry, though. I've come to terms with this new way of things. It sure beats the old "Sleep War" days. So here's to comfort objects:

Too Many Toys in the Bed

The mom of a toddler once said,
"He has too many toys in his bed.
Every time he gets in, he adds seven or ten.
He has too many toys in his bed.

"These toys are not snuggly or plush,
But he gathers them up in a rush.
He won't give up one and has far too much fun
With too many toys in his bed.

"The bedtime routine we've got down,
But skip this one step and he'll frown.
After I sing, he says 'I want to bring
Another new toy to my bed!'

"When he moves the toys jingle and clink.
That cannot be comfy, I think.
Though he's well-loved and fed, he will scream himself red
'Til he has all his toys in his bed.

108

"It's amazing he gets any sleep,
But he does it with nary a peep.
He feels comfort and pride with his toys by his side.
Are there too many toys in his bed?

"He sleeps soundly on train sets and blocks.
And for comfort, he snuggles pet rocks.
Try to take them, he'll cry. They stack ten stories high.
He has too many toys in his bed.

"A plastic Buzz Lightyear's a must,
And it's Star Wars light saber or bust.
He brings Thomas and Friends and Legos without end.
Oh there's too many toys in his bed.

"His tricycle helmet's there too.
The child even brings the odd shoe,
And a wooden cork gun. It all must weigh a ton.
He has too many toys in his bed.

"Between naptimes I sneak out a few,
But he finds them and adds them anew.
So with hands in the air, I try not to care
About too many toys in his bed."

A PROMISE

"Correct your son, and he will give you rest; yes he will give delight to your soul" (Proverbs 29:17).

109

A PRAYER

God of rest, I thank You for giving me the discipline to teach my son how to sleep. Thank You for walking with me through the valley of our struggles, for granting me the perseverance to follow through with the lessons I teach, and for greeting me on the other end of our journey with a reassuring smile. Help me find delight in my soul for each new development I experience in this journey with my child.

My *Other* Children

I haven't told you much about my *other* children. Despite all the warnings I'd received from well-intentioned and dead-on correct family members, I rushed to get a dog soon after Adel and I got married. My Pomeranian, Bitsy, became my first "child." I hauled Bitsy and her entourage of toys and gadgets everywhere I went. It was a little insane, I confess. But worry not, reader! Just like everything else in my life, my relationship with dogs changed dramatically with the birth of my first *real* child. In short, once I had kids, my dogs became dogs.

In the beginning, Bitsy was a wildly energetic puppy, ripping off all the book covers on the bottom shelves, destroying everything in her path. Her destruction culminated in one disgustingly explosive disaster. We were preparing for a camping trip and had left a bag of food supplies on the bar stools while we went to work. When we returned home to pack up our supplies and head out, we learned what Bitsy had been up to in our absence.

On the floor of the kitchen was a torn paper bag that had contained all our camping grocery supplies. Partially eaten graham crackers, chocolate bars, hot dog buns, and marshmallows were scattered, crumbled and gooey, all over the kitchen floor. It was amazing to find how little of the brand new packages still remained intact. The amount of damage caused by a dog so small was astounding. She must have eaten more than her weight in camping cuisine. What a feat of consumption! But wait…there's more!

Apparently, after eating most of our weekend's dry food rations, Bitsy had run into a "bit" of a tummy ache. Here's where we get to the "explosive disaster" part. I discovered the carnage everywhere. Apparently she had been projectile spraying out of both ends for quite some time. The furniture, floor, and walls were smattered and smeared with congealed brownish goo, in some places as high up as three feet! Oh how I wish I had placed a hidden video camera in our house that day. Or maybe I'm really glad I didn't. Gross.

No worries though. After hours of scrubbing and contemplating a pet emergency room visit (me) or assisted suicide (Adel) we decided to let Bitsy's self-inflicted torture run its course and she turned out fine. We still went camping after another trip to the grocery store and only had to take Bitsy to the animal hospital one time that weekend for eating something poisonous at the campsite which left her tipsy and staggering until she retched it up onto the floor of the car. Good times. Good times. We moved out of that rental home shortly after the explosive-camping-food episode and it was condemned and torn down shortly after. I'm serious.

Not long after the camping incident, we (I) decided that we had not yet had enough of the doggy-filled pleasures of life, so we adopted another Pomeranian named Prancer. He was calm, gentle, and sweet. Everyone loved him except for his slightly disturbing habit of backing his rear end right into you. Unfortunately, Prancer died just after a year with us, in spite of our exce$$ive efforts to save him. We vowed never again to pour absurd gobs of money into attempting to save a dog's life (sorry Bitsy!).

This would have been the perfect time to slim down our responsibilities by keeping it to one dog. I was already pregnant with Isaac and planning to quit my job in a few months. However, this information didn't seem to factor in to my "logic" when I considered adopting another pet. After one visit to a local shelter, we (I) picked out Molly. She seemed like a perfect replacement for Prancer, cuddly and calm in contrast to Bitsy's jittery enthusiasm.

I knew it was a mistake the first day I brought her home. I learned quickly that Molly's apparent cuddly and calm demeanor was a mask for her true clingy and cloying personality. She found it necessary to be touching a human at all times. When I was able to coerce her out the back door, she would sit at the door whining until I let her back in to pee on my rug. What she really needed were owners who would let her snuggle on their laps even while they sat on the toilet. We never gelled with Molly, but we tried to make this unlikely dog a member of our family.

The family dynamic changed quite a bit once we had Isaac. When I came home from the hospital, I was so overwhelmed with caring for my new baby that I didn't even want to touch my dogs, who were scrambling for my attention. It was as if the limited amount of affection I had to give was overly-consumed by the constant needs of my infant. I have a photograph of Bitsy and Molly lying on their bellies, noses pushed under the bedroom door, pining away for me as I secluded myself in the room to nurse Isaac. The dogs still lived plush and cushy lives, but they had lost their position as "children" in our household. By the time we had Abby the attitude was, "Sorry dogs, but your needs are on the bottom of the totem pole and the pole is getting taller."

While we spent the first six months of Abby's life learning to meet the needs of a toddler and a newborn, we were also juggling the status quo of the dogs. They required two walks a day or Molly would pee on my new carpets. We were begrudgingly keeping up when it slowly began to dawn on us that maybe we should try to find a new,

113

loving home for Molly. I put an ad out, being completely honest about her age and her neediness. To my surprise I got an instant reply. It was perfect: an elderly lady who wanted a lapdog companion! I couldn't have been more pleased...until Molly got sick. Horrible timing! I couldn't give away a sick dog and a sick dog was much more than we could handle.

"Let's just run some diagnostics and at least determine what's wrong with her before you make any decisions," the veterinarian prompted.

"Okay," I relented tearfully. That made sense. They carried Molly away through the visiting room doors and then returned to show me the bill for her diagnostic tests: $263! Just for the tests! Who knows how much the treatment on top of that would cost? "Wow. This is way more than I expected," I gulped. "I need to talk to my husband first." I thought back to Prancer and our vow. I thought of sweet Molly and how hard it had been for us to love her. I thought of how I was barely managing to care for two healthy dogs, much less a sick one.

In the end, eyes swollen with grief and failure, I confessed to the veterinarian that we were not going to pay to diagnose the problem. "We don't really want this dog, anymore." I said through tears. "She has never been a good fit for our family and all this is more than we can handle right now." The words were out. I had admitted, out loud, to being a failure of the dog-rescue system. I had adopted a dog I couldn't keep. I, new mother of two, was a betrayer of dog-lovers everywhere.

The vet handled my betrayal well, considering that she makes it her profession to care for and love animals. Much to my relief the vet offered for the clinic to adopt Molly from us. Once I signed papers relinquishing all our rights of ownership of Molly, they would be able to diagnose and treat her, hopefully to a complete recovery. Then they would find a new home for her. I hope that Molly is well and has found her perfect owner.

Bitsy couldn't have cared less that Molly didn't return home with me. Isaac asked about her from time to time but did not mourn her absence. Adel was relieved that he did not have any more exce$$ive veterinary bills to pay. Abby was completely unaware of the proceedings. And I felt conflicted.

I felt the weight of guilt for my failure but also a great sense of relief. I was sorry that I had failed the system of caring for animals that need safe, loving homes. I was relieved to have one less creature to care for when my days were overwhelming and my nights too short. I was sad that I failed a sweet, needy dog named Molly. And, while there was no clear right answer in this scenario, I was relieved that putting the needs of my family first helped to bring the blessing of peace to our home.

A PROMISE

"And we know that all things work together for good to those who love God, to those who are the called according to His purpose" (Romans 8:28).

A PRAYER

God, You know the guilt that I feel over my failures. It is painful when I'm forced to acknowledge that despite all my efforts, I'm still missing the mark. But it is a good reminder that I need You. I pray that You work this situation into good. Use it to teach me, to shape me, and to grow me into Your likeness.

Food Court

Often at the conclusion of an outing with my children, I feel that I have survived a great ordeal. Sometimes getting them from one location to the next is like wrestling two grisly bears to the floor. Sometimes stopping the incessant noise from their mouths is like warding off swarms of locusts as they pelt into my head. Today we went to the mall to spend the gift cards I received for Christmas. I know that shopping with two kids is no fun. Actually, I can accurately state that with *my* two kids it's quite impossible. But I'm no fool, so I asked Mimi to come along to help.

Even with the extra pair of hands, shopping with my children is hard work. Isaac enjoys sitting in his stroller for about 0.3 seconds and only when it's in motion. If we stop to look at anything he tries to make a break for it. Abby, at six months old, is so mellow and easy-going that she is no trouble at all except that she needs you to replenish her snack or toy supply that she drops to the ground about every minute and a half.

Still, somehow I managed to use Adel's gift card to get him some nice new shirts. I spent mine on a new pair of shoes. Then we ate lunch. That seems simple enough but for some reason it's just not. There should be an instruction manual for outings like this.

How to Eat a Meal at a Mall Food Court with One Toddler and One Baby:

- Stand in line.
- Order low-quality food.
- Pay much more than it's worth.
- Sit down.
- Plunk toddler in chair.
- Check chicken nuggets for scalding danger.
- Squeeze ketchup for nuggets.
- Open milk.
- Return to counter to get straw.
- Rummage through diaper bag.
    - Retrieve rice cereal, spoon, and bib.
- Put bib on baby.
- Set out mommy food.
- Get up.
    - Supervise toddler's clean up of french fries from floor.
    - Tell toddler to stop eating food off the ground.
    - Plunk toddler back down in chair.
- Sit down.
- Simultaneously feed baby and self.
    - Bite for baby.
    - Bite for mommy.
    - Bite for baby.
    - Bite for…Look under the table for toddler's toy that fell.
- Kick toy toward toddler so he can reach it.

- Grab toddler's arm to restrain from un-chaperoned mall exploration.
- Wipe toddler's hands and face.
- Restrain toddler in stroller harness.
- Ignore toddler's pleas for freedom.
- Wrestle slimy spoon from baby's hand.
- Resume eating.
  - Bite for baby.
  - Bite for mommy.
  - Bite for baby.
  - Bite for mommy.
- Wipe baby's hands and face.
- Wipe baby's hands and face and hair.
- Tell toddler to stop screaming.
- Throw away all trash items.
- Cram all baby essentials back into diaper bag.
- Avoid eye contact with nearby diners.
- Make hasty exit.
- Sigh.
- Give thanks for surviving another meal.

Thus passes another "enjoyable" meal with both kids. I'm relieved to have survived it. And all of this was with Mimi's extra pair of hands. After our meal, I tell my mom my thoughts on our dining experience. Everything feels like chaos and survival. She tells me that she always struggled with that too as a mom. Now as a grandma, she tries to consciously remind herself that, although it can be crazy, *this* is what it's all about. In the tough moments, she encouraged me to imagine what life would be like without my children. That thought sobered me up real quick. I'll take chaos any day.

Yes, it is so worth it.

A PROMISE

"Where no oxen are, the trough is clean; but much increase comes by the strength of an ox" (Proverbs 14:4).

A PRAYER

Lord, my little cattle sure make for a messy trough. I am forever cleaning up after them. But what these small creatures add to my life is even more astounding than the messes they make or the trouble they cause. They are capable, just by being who they are, of bringing me so much joy. Thank You, thank You, God, for my children.

I Can't Find My Brain

My brain has officially abandoned ship. I've heard women claim this after the birth of their first child, or even during pregnancy, but I never really experienced the so-called "mommy brain" like I am right now. I'm forgetful and disorganized and I can't focus on one thing for more than a minute.

Today I returned home from an outing only to find I'd forgotten to close the garage door. It was gaping open all morning, inviting everyone in through our unlocked back entrance. I also misplace things frequently. Last week, I put the peanut butter in the refrigerator and the milk in the cupboard. And where are my keys? For the millionth time, I have no idea. If they're not in the top three most-likely locations, it's hopeless.

I had another experience recently that further illustrates how my brain is clearly Missing In Action. On this particular day, I was calling my husband at work to tell him, just twenty minutes before his appointment, the address of the doctor's office. I was supposed to give him this information the night before...then in the morning...by this time it was nearly too late.

(For a realistic reading of the following paragraph, read it as fast as you can, in one breath, and while frantically trying to search online for the map to the doctor's office that you were supposed to give your husband yesterday.)

"I'm sorry I'm calling so late...The last thirty minutes have been crazy!...We got home from our mommy group playdate and I had to get both kids ready for their naps...After I changed Isaac's diaper, I changed Abby's diaper...While I was changing Abby, Isaac pooped in his new, clean diaper so I had to change him again...Then we went upstairs and Abby played while I read Isaac a few books, got him a drink of water, and sang him a song in bed...As I picked up Abby to leave Isaac's room and nurse her for her naptime, I smelled that her diaper was now dirty again too...But hers was a HUGE blowout diaper so I had to bring her downstairs, strip off her clothes, and put her in the bath...I was washing Abby's pants in the sink and watching her as she sat playing in the tub in an inch or two of water...Naturally, she fell over, bonked her head, and started crying...I quickly rinsed her off and got her dressed while she was still very upset...But she calmed down when I gave her Isaac's toy flute to play with...Then I brought her upstairs again to nurse her and put her in her crib...I just got back downstairs to look up the address and call you...Anyway, the address is 244 Medical Center Boulevard...You have to leave right away to get there in time....What?...You don't think your appointment is at two o'clock?...You think it's at half past two?...Let me check...Let's see...Oh, you're right!...Well that's good...Now you can take your time getting there...Oh my gosh, I need a vacation."

Thus passes another day in the life of a scatterbrained mom.

I was going to write something else here and it was really funny, but now I can't remember what it was. No, I'm not senile; I'm a mother of two.

I hope I find my brain soon because it's really hard being me right now.

A PROMISE

"For God is not the author of confusion but of peace, as in all the churches of the saints" (1 Corinthians 14:33).

A PRAYER

Lord, I praise You that You are the Author of peace and not the Author of my overwhelming confusion. To say that I'm a little confused right now would be a gross understatement. I'm scatterbrained, unreliable, forgetful, absent-minded. And what I need right now more than anything is Your peace. I need peace in the crazy days, peace for my striving, and peace for my frazzled mind. I confess that it is a struggle for me to sit still and let You bless me with Your peace. I pray that You will teach me how I can let You fill me up.

Messin' With Texas

A PERSPECTIVE

I know it's not a good idea to "mess with Texas" but I have to mess with it just a little bit since it has been my new home for over a year now and it is a great deal more comical to me than California ever was. Actually, I love everything about my new home except the weather and the bugs. Okay, I love everything about Texas except the weather and the bugs *and* the obsession with firearms. I recently came across a car ad in the local newspaper. This local used-car dealership is advertising that their customers will, and I quote, "Receive a free handgun with the purchase of any car!" What an amazing deal! Even more amazing is that the same dealership will provide "A free 12 Gauge Shotgun with the purchase of any New or Used SUV!" I'm not sure if this firearm-phenomenon occurs in other states, but I can honestly say it has made a true impression on me of the character of my new home state. (Love it.)

Then there's the weather. As a Southern California dweller, I am not accustomed to having to consider the weather into my plans. In much of the Golden State, you can plan an event at a park a month in advance with near certainty that it will be a nice sunny day. Thus the reason why everyone wants to live there and it costs more for a one bedroom condominium than you will ever make in your lifetime, even *if* you sell your first-born child on e-Bay. In Texas, since we live close to the Gulf Coast, I live in near-constant fear of a hurricane or tornado. Any little breeze sends me checking the weather radio for a killer storm. I think I prefer to take my chances with California's earthquakes. Earthquakes give you no warning so there's really nothing to be afraid of other than instant death or dismemberment. The only thing predictable about Texas weather is the relentless, steadfast, and unfailing torture of the hot and humid summer months. It feels like we're all bathing in the armpit of a marathon runner who is on his eighteenth mile. Nice, huh?

Lastly, we have had to learn quickly that the bugs are at the top of the food chain here. Fire ants are a lovely breed of ants that dwell everywhere your children want to play. Some friends of ours from California who used to reside in Texas warned us about them. They made the ants sound so scary, warning of the danger to infants and the elderly who cannot move fast enough to escape the swarming armies. But I figured these ants were to be found in more rural areas and our corner of suburbia would be quite safe from the spectacle. Not so. Here in the great state of Texas there is a fire ant mound roughly every four-and-a-half feet. They are piles of dirt that look like loosely ground sawdust. Thing is, once you step on a mound, it takes about three seconds before every ant in the vicinity comes furiously racing up from underground tunnels to repeatedly bite you on your offending appendage.

Recently we learned the hard way that Isaac is allergic to fire ant bites. The four of us were walking around the block in our usual evening routine. I was carrying Abby and holding Bitsy's leash while Isaac and Adel walked behind. Suddenly I heard Isaac saying, "It hurts, it hurts, it hurts." He was bending down brushing his hands over his feet as Adel stood looking at him curiously. I dropped Bitsy's leash, set Abby down on the sidewalk (thankful she can now safely sit up unsupported) and ran back toward Isaac. Quickly I picked him up and brushed off as many ants as I could see. Then I removed his shoes and clothing to check for more ants, all the while scolding Adel for his lack of response (my husband is a wonderful father but sometimes *ugh* is all I can say!).

When we got home I assessed the damage. I could see a dozen or so bites on his feet and ankles and a few going up his legs. The bites were already beginning to swell and Isaac was complaining, rubbing and scratching his legs. I plunked him down in the cool water of the bathtub which seemed to provide some temporary relief. Then I checked his body again, afraid that I had missed something. To my horror, this time he appeared to have bites all over his diaper area too. I wondered if I had failed to remove a stray ant from his diaper that had enjoyed a glorious heyday of revenge by biting him over and over again.

After the bath, we went upstairs to play but Isaac kept rubbing and itching and was clearly agitated. Oddly, this time he was rubbing his back and chest as well as his bottom and legs. I checked once again and saw bites going all the way up his sides to his neck. *Surely I am going crazy*, I thought. I was so angry at Adel for not helping Isaac sooner. How did he get fire ant bites all the way up to his neck? Finally I called the nurse-line provided by Isaac's pediatrician. She told me to watch his breathing and prescribed Benadryl and a topical cream which I immediately sent Adel to gather from the store.

I checked on Isaac several times throughout the night to make sure his breathing was normal. In the morning, most of the bumps were gone and the ones on his ankles were already turning into the usual pimple-like pustules of day-old fire ant bites. It was then that I realized that the bumps, which had appeared the night before to be growing up Isaac's sides, were actually hives and not bites. This discovery was accompanied by a mix of relief and worry. I felt relief that it was not my neglect that had allowed for more ant bites than I had originally thought. But I also felt worry because if the ant bites resulted in hives this time, it could be possible that future bites would lead to the respiratory problems the nurse had warned about.

Since then, we have had no problem with the fire ants. Isaac, who used to put up a big fight to be allowed to tromp dangerously through the grass, now believes me when I say to watch out for ant hills. You should see that boy run over the grass when he has to cross it. I am quite well-trained now at spotting the notorious mounds. So well, in fact, that on a recent trip to California, I couldn't help but do my protective scan as we walked through the park.

We still enjoy our evening walks around the block but the ants never let us forget we live in Texas now. That, and the neighbor who, upon seeing Isaac running to keep up with Bitsy while he held onto her leash, hollered across the street at us: "Looks like yer dawg is walkin' yer boy." Yup, we live in Texas now.

A PROMISE

"Where can I go from Your Spirit? Or where can I flee from Your presence? If I ascend into heaven, You are there; if I make my bed in hell, behold, You are there. If I take the wings of the morning, and dwell in the uttermost parts of the sea, even there Your hand shall lead me, and Your right hand shall hold me" (Psalm 139:7-10).

A PRAYER

Lord, my new home is not exactly the uttermost parts of the sea, but it nevertheless contains strange and unexpected qualities. It is always difficult adjusting to a new place, and my difficulty adjusting here is compounded by my struggles over the past several months to create order in my new-found chaos. It comforts me, God, to know that here or anywhere else I may choose to go, You are with me.

Child-Proof

Every night Adel and I pray that God will protect our children. It's a good thing too because this world is a dangerous place and small children work very hard at trying to destroy themselves.

Experienced parents know that there are several indispensible phrases that had better become a part of your daily vocabulary:

- Don't eat that!
- Get down from there!
- Put that back!
- Don't hit!
- Get out of the toilet!
- Medicine is NOT candy!
- Put your sister down!
- Electrical outlets are not toys!
- Put the saw back in the garage!

And that's just for starters. I spend a great deal of time checking and double checking to make sure my kids stay safe. I buy all the child-proofing gadgets recommended by mothers and pediatricians around the world. And I maintain strict safety policies such as "children can only drive the car when it is not really in motion." So you see, I work very hard to keep my kids safe.

Sadly, in other ways, *I* actually pose one of the greatest dangers to my own children. The danger from me is never intentional. I would never deliberately harm my own children. The horrible, lurking truth of the matter is that I sometimes make careless mistakes! From talking to other parents, I know I'm not alone here. The sad reality is that none of us are perfect. Until we are, there's always the chance we will make a mistake that will endanger our children.

Okay, I promised you the gritty truth in this book, so here it is. These are the confessions of an imperfect mom:

Confession #1

I frequently laid newborn Abby on the couch and left her unattended for a few minutes. I did this often enough that eventually she rolled off with a thud. There were tears on her part, and tremendous feelings of guilt on my part as the cautions of the doctors, grandmas, and advice-givers of the world played over and over again in my head. All new mothers know The Rule so well we can all say it unison: "Never leave the baby unattended on an elevated surface!" I'd like to add a personal note-to-self: "You idiot!" She's okay now, I think, but when she doesn't get into Yale, we'll know why.

Confession #2

Also, with *both* of my kids (but on separate occasions), I have driven the long drive from my house to my mom's house only to realize that, for whatever reason, I never actually buckled them into their car seats.

Confession #3

And finally, I accidentally dropped two-year-old Isaac, face down, in a parking lot. You see, I have been toting my two children around by putting Abby in the stroller and sitting Isaac up on the handlebars. Really, since he has an aversion to sitting still, he's rarely even in the stroller at all. So this method works...*kind of.* What I didn't realize at first was that it was merely Abby's weight in the front of the stroller that kept Isaac from tipping the whole thing over. This is, of course, what happened. As I absentmindedly picked Abby up one day, I heard a man's voice yell out in a thick southern drawl: "Oh no you *didn't!*" He ran over almost in time to catch Isaac before he slammed face first into the asphalt. As if I didn't feel rotten enough, I then had to comfort my son while being scolded by a man with missing teeth (maybe his mother did the same thing to him?). Yes, it was a dark day in my life as a parent. Thankfully Isaac wasn't hurt. Not even a scratch. Naturally, he was scared, but he did forgive me.

As much as I try to keep my kids safe, the truth of the matter is that sometimes my own efforts are not enough. Inevitably, I'm going to make mistakes. That's the truly scary part. I'm human and I'm in charge of protecting these delicate, beautiful children. I have been forced to realize that, as much as I long to do everything perfectly, that's just not going to happen. Sometimes I am my own worst enemy.

As a mom, I have my soul so intensely entwined in the existence of my children, so much so that I would rather die a thousand deaths than have anything bad happen to them. When I fail, or when their safety is beyond my control, the dreadful "what-ifs" come raging into my most fearful thoughts.

That's why Adel and I pray every night together that God will protect our babies. God wants us to be responsible for the blessings He has given us. He wants me to do my best to control what I can in terms of keeping my children safe. He wants me to double check, dot all my

I's, cross all my T's. But He also wants me to know that ultimately, these babies are His children too.

The deepest reality is that they are *His* most precious treasures even more than they are mine. *He* created them. *He* loves them with a more perfect and selfless love than I could ever imagine. More important even than my daily prayers asking for protection, is the daily reminder that these children are *His* children. God asks me to daily release to Him that which I hold most dear, trusting Him to be their ultimate Gentle Shepherd. And in the moments when I realize that I've messed up and compromised what I hold most dear, I thank God for His intervention and protection.

A PROMISE

"For He shall give His angels charge over you, to keep you in all your ways. In their hands they shall bear you up, lest you dash your foot against a stone" (Psalm 91:11-12).

A PRAYER

Father of us all, I pray that You would continue to protect my children, especially in my moments of failure. I know You love my children even more than I do (although I admit that's hard to imagine!). They are *Your* precious babies as well as mine and I willingly and completely entrust them to Your hands.

130

Sleep?

4:14AM

The first thing that reaches me through the depths of my sleep is the sound. Initially, Abby's coos actually enter my dream and become part of the psychedelic atmosphere. But they persist and eventually my brain is pulled through the fog and into the darkness of my bedroom, where I realize I'm hearing Abby over the monitor. She is awake and playing in her bed.

I stay still for a while, listening. She's not crying, just making noise, and I'd rather have her put herself back to sleep if she can.

4:32AM

The cooing is beginning to alternate with whimpers and cries. This whole time I have been in a near-sleep state, listening to Abby play. Every time my mind relaxes back into the fog again, Abby's persistent monolog interrupts, pulling me back into consciousness. It's like the Navy Seal "hell week" documentary I saw a while ago where the potential Seals huddle on a dark beach, feet in cold water all night long. When someone, despite the discomfort and cold, starts to drift

131

off to sleep, one of the drill sergeants yells and prods him with end of his rifle. At least that's how I feel each time Abby cries out and jerks me from near sleep.

As for Adel, in his robot-like calculations, he hears her sounds, acknowledges my existence, and rolls over, back into his deep sleep. I can picture his mind assessing the situation like "The Terminator:"

`Baby: crying…`

`Woman: able to help…`

`Terminator: back into hibernate mode.`

Thanks for the help, dear.

4:36AM

Abby is no longer intermittently cooing. Rather, the crying has become persistent enough that I decide she's beyond putting herself back to sleep. I groan, as I stumble my way upstairs to her door. But as I approach the door, I realize I'm not hearing her anymore. Perhaps she finally did fall asleep as I made my way upstairs? I listen to the silence for a minute and decide to take my chances and return to my bed. If she is finally starting to fall asleep, the last thing she needs is me butting in and reinforcing her dependence.

4:38AM

I'm not sure why she was silent while I was upstairs, but as soon as I settle into my bed again, she starts to cry intensely. At least I wasn't asleep again yet. So, it's back upstairs to find her binky (she takes one now…hooray!), snuggle her in her blanket, and hum for a few minutes as she relaxes her head into my neck. As I lay her back down, she starts to cry, but I leave the room anyway, stopping outside the door to listen. I really want her to go back to sleep without nursing, knowing it's a bad habit to start, considering that, at seven months old, she's been sleeping through the night for months now.

After a minute of intense crying that would break my heart if I weren't so tired, she settles down into her bed and is still.

4:46AM

I have once again settled myself into bed in the silence of the darkest hour before dawn. My mind has been too stimulated to fall immediately into sleep but it's beginning to relax. Then I hear Abby's newest round of intense wailing. She must have been trying, but was unable, to fall asleep. "Oh, for crying out loud!" I grumble into the darkness, secretly glad that Adel's movements imply that Abby and I have woken him up. At least I'm not suffering alone. Then I wonder, with irony, if the phrase "for crying out loud" actually originated from a situation like this.

I throw the covers back dramatically as I stomp back up the stairs, careful my stomping is controlled enough not to wake Isaac too and double my trouble. I enter Abby's room and put on motherly compassion like a robe, picking up my crying child with reassurance and taking her to my breast where she instantly relaxes into peace. She wins. Now I wish I had just gone up and nursed her at the first little coo. We would have both been asleep instead of awake this whole time. At least now she doesn't cry as I settle her back into her crib.

4:53AM

As I flop myself back under my own covers to attempt sleep once again, Adel begins to stir. After having his own sleep interrupted by his wife and child so many times, he has finally given up and decides to get up for the day and shower. *Great timing*, I think to myself, anticipating that each little sound he makes as he's getting ready is going to keep me from falling back asleep. I wonder if it's revenge for my earlier glee at disturbing his sleep. I listen to the shower running for a while, piling pillows on top of my head to block out the noises around me. Then I stop noticing and the fog wins.

133

A PROMISE

"Come to Me, all you who labor and are heavy laden, and I will give you rest" (Matthew 11:28).

A PRAYER

Rest. Lord, You know well how we long for rest when it is scarce. I have had many short, interrupted nights since having children. These nights can be grueling and torturous but somehow I also manage to cherish the quietness in which I am blessed to tend to the needs of my little ones. It is a burden, but not a heavy one. Still, I want to turn to You for the rest I often cannot find. Bless me with rest, Lord!

Dinosaur Bloopers

Right now scientists all over the world are in really hot water with me. For one thing, you would think that people with a job title such as "paleontologist" would have a few grains of common sense rattling around in their heads. Perhaps they lost what grains they had while combing through vast wastelands, such as Texas, in search of giant fossilized bones.

Here's what's gotten me so frustrated with those "specialists in paleontology:" they messed the whole thing up for two year olds! I mean, didn't they think, for just one moment, that perhaps rough and tumble two-year-old boys might find gigantic, ferocious reptiles fascinating?

You're still thinking about it?

Well, the answer is no. Of course they didn't think of that, which is why dinosaurs have such arduously, impossibly, laboriously difficult names to pronounce.

Isaac has a dinosaur book that's way too old for him but he likes to look at the pictures and point to each one, innocently asking what it's called. Actually, I think he does it because he secretly knows I can't really pronounce any of them and he thinks it's funny to hear me stumble through:

Isaac: Mom, what's that one's name?

Mommy: Let's see. That's the Tyrannosaurus Rex.

Isaac: T-Rex. (*he corrects me*) What's this one called?

Mommy: That's the Archaeornithomimus.

Isaac: This one?

Mommy: Well, that is clearly the Chungkingosaurus.

Isaac: What are those ones called?

Mommy: Those are the Muttaburrasaurus, the Eustreptospondylus, and the Saurornitholestes.

I might as well be saying "bleh-bleh-bleh-bleh" but he giggles as I fumble each ridiculous name. If you think I am making up the names, check it out online. These names are *for real* and my child likes to make me say them on a daily basis. There are hundreds more names like these that scientists clearly thought up for the sole purpose of aggravating the parents of small children. Whatever happened to simple names for animals like "dog" and "cow"?

While we're bashing scientists, let's add one more log to the fire. Whatever happened to the Brontosaurus? Along with the T. Rex and the Triceratops, he was one of my childhood favorites and one of the few whose pronunciation I've mastered. I have been doing some serious study on this subject and consequently have become, in the course of my twenty minutes of research, an ardent and prominent "messupologist" (one who studies scientific bloopers). It helps that I am actually the only messupologist in the entire history of the universe, having completely fabricated the term.

In my extensive messupology research on a highly questionable website, I discovered that the term "Brontosaurus" was actually a case of mistaken identity. One so-called "paleontologist" came across some bones out in the wilderness somewhere and believed he had discovered a new species of dinosaur, thus naming it Brontosaurus (which, according to my laborious research derives from the Greek words *bronto* and *saurus*, meaning "Brontosaurus"). It was the largest fossilized skeleton found at that time so the Brontosaurus became quite well known.

In actuality what the man found was just a larger version of the Apatosaurus. So, the scientific community, without telling anyone, secretly stopped using the term "Brontosaurus." Instead they started snickering behind the backs of the average, everyday humans who ignorantly continued to use that term. And they're doing it again right now to all those schmucks among us who still name Pluto as one of the planets! (Don't feel bad, I would too if my husband weren't a rocket scientist, forever drilling useless facts into my head!)

But back to dinosaurs. For a few years as a child, I was fascinated with dinosaurs. Determined to be a paleontologist myself, I saved my allowance and ordered a set of "high-quality plastic" dinosaurs from a catalog. As I grew older, those dinosaurs were passed around in my family tree until last year when they ended up back in my living room for Isaac to play with. In among the other dinosaurs, painted red and green, is the one I used to call "Brontosaurus." In fact, the word "Brontosaurus" is etched on his plastic underbelly. When Isaac asks me what his name is, I don't really know what to tell him. If it's not a Brontosaurus, is it an Apatosaurus, a Diplodocus, a Brachiosaurus, or is it something else entirely?

137

I say let's just call him "Billy."

A PROMISE

"Where is the wise? Where is the scribe? Where is the disputer of this age? Has not God made foolish the wisdom of this world?" (1 Corinthians 1:20).

A PRAYER

Lord, the wisdom of the earth that I teach my children today may be found foolishness tomorrow. But Your wisdom is everlasting. It never changes. I love that there is stability and true wisdom in following You! I pray that my children will learn to discern Your constant wisdom from the ever-changing wisdom of the world.

Midnight Mouse

A PERSPECTIVE

Last night I was abruptly awakened from my sleep by Isaac screaming. My dreams were such that a rude wake up call was actually a bit of a relief. I rushed upstairs to comfort him and that's when I learned that the book *If You Give a Mouse a Cookie* is actually prophetic.

Those mommas who have never read *If You Give a Mouse a Cookie* by Laura Joffe Numeroff (try saying *that* three times fast) should run out right now and buy six copies. Or we could all just give Ms. Numeroff gobs of money because she is clearly a great and powerful prophet. But, you see, the prophecy is a metaphor. The way it works is that the *mouse* is actually *your child* and the *cookie* is *whatever it happens to be that your child is asking for at two in the morning.* What follows the cookie in Numeroff's story is that the conniving mouse asks for one thing after the next from the little boy, who never questions why the mouse should get his every demand met. That is precisely what happened on this particular night between my own little mouse and me.

In this case, the *cookie* was *to hold him.* He was terrified of something and all he would say was, "Lego men." Naturally, this led me to believe that he had either had a bad dream about Lego men, or he had finally been poked awake by one of the dozen little fellows that he brought to bed last night. So, just like the boy in the book who constantly gets manipulated into fulfilling little mouse-whims, I picked Isaac up and held him.

But my little mouse was not finished with me yet. Once I held him, he wanted me to sing a song. Then, before I returned him to his bed, he wanted some milk. As we came downstairs to get the milk, he wanted to see Daddy. So we woke up Daddy just so the little mouse could say hello.

After visiting Daddy, I tried to steer his mind back towards sleep:

Me: Isaac, do you see how dark it is?

Isaac: Yes.

Me: It's dark because the sun is down and the moon is up.

Isaac: The moon is up?

Me: Yes. That means it's sleep time!

Isaac: I want to see the moon!

At that point I was wide awake myself, so I thought, *what the heck, let's go look at the moon for a minute.* It seemed like a good teaching moment. Well the moon was not out at this particular time. But we did see some pretty stars. A few minutes later, when I finally had snuggled him into bed, he was quite content and ready to sleep.

As for me, I tossed and turned for the next hour, unable to fall asleep until well past three in the morning. Then my *other* mouse woke me up at five. This one is the *little girl* mouse whose face is still yellow from the food coloring her big brother poured on her head yesterday afternoon. Ever since last week when I caved and nursed her out of schedule at 4:46AM, Abby has been waking up before six in the morning to nurse. That's her cookie. And, as we all know, if you give a mouse a cookie…

A PROMISE

"If a son asks for bread from any father among you, will he give him a stone? Or if he asks for a fish, will he give him a serpent instead of a fish? Or if he asks for an egg, will he offer him a scorpion? If you then, being evil, know how to give good gifts to your children, how much more will your heavenly Father give the Holy Spirit to those who ask Him!" (Luke 11:11-13).

A PRAYER

God, I cannot help but give good things to my children and they cannot help but ask for them. Sometimes we get a little carried away, them with asking and me with giving! But I know the desire I have to provide for my children comes from You. As my loving Father, I ask that You give me Your Holy Spirit so that I may have wisdom in handling the concerns of my children.

A God's Eye View

I have been plagued on and off with acne since I was a teenager. I recently read that "most people" grow out of acne troubles by the time they become adults. There is only a tiny percentage of adults that continue to suffer from chronic acne. Lucky me, I'm one of them!

During both of my pregnancies my skin was the clearest it had been since before puberty. I loved it. But after those preggo hormones faded away, the zit-producing glands got back to work. Hi-ho! Every pore on my face is now angry and has something to say about it. And because I'm nursing Abby, I can't even use any powerful defenses. My doctor wants me to wait until I've weaned Abby before I engage in a pharmaceutical pimple-war. I nursed Isaac for a full year and I plan to do the same with Abby, acne or no acne. So I wait.

Let me set the record straight: in spite of my choice to temporarily live with it...I *hate* acne. I'm not aiming to win any beauty pageants here. I just want to look clean and decent. I do not enjoy the constant fear that the giant zit on my cheek might poke someone's eye out, or worse, that it might develop a personality of its own and start trying to undermine my attempts at making new friends. *Pssst,* the giant zit would say to the new mommy friend I just met. *Pssst! Did you know that Megan actually lets her kids eat the food that falls on the floor? And she doesn't even care if the dog chews on the baby's toys! Plus, look at me! I'm a big, talking zit right on her cheek! This woman is clearly not a suitable friend for you!* My potential "new friend" would back away slowly, corralling her small children behind her for protection as she left.

When I have bad skin, I am conscious of it all the time. I want to stay in my house and hide. I probably would if all my pores held their mutiny at the same time, allowing me to wait out the onslaught. But often it lasts for months on end, with each individual gland waging its own private battle against my ego. I can't give up my new friends and social life for months at a time just because I feel ugly. Usually when I'm feeling this way, I'll try to compensate for my ugly skin by wearing earrings and makeup. My hope is that if my earrings are distracting enough, or my lashes long enough, people won't see the four giant zits singing in unison on my chin or the large red bump in the middle of my forehead that's trying to strike up its own inappropriate conversation in spite of my best efforts to talk over it.

Recently, as I was in the throes of acne wars with my face and truly feeling icky, God used seven-month-old Abby to remind me how much I am loved. It was afternoon and Abby had just woken from her nap. While Isaac remained asleep, I crept downstairs with Abby so that we could have some mother-daughter time. As the groggy expression faded away from her eyes, Abby suddenly looked up at my face. What she did then made me truly feel love and acceptance the way God intends it. She looked at my face, sprinkled with the red bumps that constantly cripple my ego. Then, looking past all the blemishes, she smiled into my eyes. Her tiny hand reached up and caressed my cheek and her cupid mouth curved brightly as she gazed at me. Her expression was one of recognition, of love, of adoration. She did not care that I felt (or looked) ugly. Truly, she did not even know about the difference between ugliness and beauty. All she knew was that here was her mother. Here was the one that she loved more than anything. Here was safety, home, nourishment, and tenderness.

With one touch and one smile, Abby reminded me that our relationship transcends my appearance just as it transcends my mood, my insecurity, my vanity, or my failures. I will always be her mother. She will always love me and I will always love her. Even more so, God will always love us both, zits and all. Just like my baby girl, God does not see my blemishes. He sees me as His pure and perfect child. If only, if only, I could always see myself through their eyes! Imagine what a wonderful and different world it would be if we were all capable of seeing ourselves and each other this way. Once Abby is fully weaned I plan to engage in full-fledged chemical warfare with my acne. Until then, I can rest in the blessed assurance that I am uncommonly and unconditionally loved.

A PROMISE

"...For the Lord does not see as man sees; for man looks at the outward appearance, but the Lord looks at the heart" (1 Samuel 16:7).

A PRAYER

Lord, thank You for helping me to see myself through Your eyes. Thank You for the blessing of my children who remind me how much You love me, even though I am flawed. Please help me to see myself this way too.

Mutton Busting

This weekend we went to the Houston Livestock Show and Rodeo. Since Abby and Isaac are still so little we decided to pass on the actual rodeo. Instead, we headed for the kiddie area, complete with pony rides, pig races, petting zoos, and carnival rides.

As luck would have it, they were beginning a new "mutton busting" competition just as we arrived. If you are a city slicker like me, you are probably wondering what in the world mutton busting is. You'll find out; just wait. We had been hearing about these competitions from Adel's coworkers and enthusiastic Texans since we moved here to the great Lone Star State. (By the way, I have never seen a state more patriotic, or I should say "state-triotic" than Texas. They have about a million songs about how great their state is, how *their* state is bigger than *your* state, and how *their* state could beat up *your* state if you dared it to. Seriously. It's very entertaining.)

Anyway, these enthusiastic Texans have been telling us about mutton busting since we arrived and we thought it sounded like a blast. As we understood it, in mutton busting you get a bunch of kids together, slap some helmets on their heads, and have them ride around on the back of sheep until they fall off. Sounds like a hoot, right?

That's what we thought. So, upon our arrival to the kiddie park at the rodeo, we were thrilled to hear that we were not too late for the competition.

The maximum age for the competition is six and the maximum weight is forty pounds (for the sheep's safety, of course), but there is no such minimum requirement in age or weight for the safety of the children. It is left up to the discretion of the parents. And we, being wholly-enthusiastic to embrace our new heritage, decided that one is never too young to start. For just ten dollars, Isaac got a blue wrist band entering him into the competition. Our excitement was building. Wouldn't it be hilarious if Isaac ended up winning? After all, he's only two and half and most of the other kids looked to be closer to four and five years old.

Isaac was thrilled at the prospect of riding a sheep and beamed proudly as the attendant buckled the helmet on his head. As we waited for the competition to begin, we looked at the sheep waiting patiently in their corral. The first thing we noticed was that these are no ordinary sheep. These sheep were more like large buffalo. They probably could hold their own quite well in one-on-one combat with the famed Texas longhorn.

As I gulped down this first hint of the kind of insanity to which I was about to submit my sweet darling child, I glanced around at the other parents. Among the clearly experienced mutton-busting crowd, one other mom in particular stood out to me. She wore the same look of belated, muted, and questioning panic that I too was struggling to suppress. And clearly by her clothes and her neatly bobbed hair, she was just as much city slicker as I was. We sympathetically gave each other a look that said, "What are we doing here?"

I made my way through the crowd of excited parents and greeted her. It turns out her son, a few months younger and quite a bit smaller than Isaac, was also entered in the competition. We had time only to briefly utter our faltering enthusiasm for this mutton busting thing, when the announcer began.

"Ladies and Gentlemen, I'd like to introduce our first competitor in this year's mutton busting competition! At thirty-six pounds and just four years old, please welcome Kyle!" As the crowd roared, the gargantuan sheep, carrying the small child on its back, was released from its corral. Within split seconds the sheep had butted, lurched, and shaken the trembling boy from its back and was now calmly munching on hay at the far side of the arena. The child, dirt and hay encrusted in every facial orifice, came hobbling out of the arena to the proud arms of his doting mother, who, seeing his tear-filled eyes and noble attempt at putting on a brave face, no doubt thumped him on the back and said, "Buck up, cowboy!"

It was about this time that Isaac turned to me and started muttering, "I don't want to. I don't want to." I was *so* relieved to hear him say that. Smart kid! However, I stalled. We had invested *ten whole dollars* into this competition. Not only that but I must admit there was a little, teeny, tiny part of me that wanted to best these locals at their own game. I mean, how proud would I be to brag about *my* son winning such a traditional Texan competition? *Maybe that sheep was especially rough*, I thought. I encouraged Isaac, and myself, to at least *watch* a few more before making any final decisions. So, we angled for a better view and watched as about three more pint-sized contestants were slammed into the padded arena walls by their ferocious vehicles.

As we watched, the urgency grew with each utterance of Isaac's "I don't want to!" If pride indeed comes before a fall, this boy wanted nothing whatsoever to do with the kind of fall those sheep were dealing. After one last-chance offer, I gratefully removed his helmet and retreated out of the contestant corral, giving an apologetic look to the other city-slicker mom who had gone white with fear.

After breathing a sigh of relief, we decided to head over to something entirely more of our pace: the pony rides. Isaac was hesitant to get on the pony at first, half expecting it to start slamming him into the wall as he had just witnessed the "docile" sheep doing to the other children. But the ride was as mundane as one would expect and we made it through, bruise-free.

Later that day, we happened to spot the other city-slicker mom and her young offspring, looking alive and well. I just had to know, so I approached and asked her how it went. Apparently her little one, like ours, inherited the cold feet of his mother. He did actually make it onto the back of his beastie before loudly voicing his change of heart, much to his father's chagrin and his mother's reprieve.

Now that we know what this so-called mutton busting is all about (*mutton* meaning "sheep" and *busting* meaning "pummeling young children"), the closest we will get in the future is the stadium seating. After all, while I don't favor my own child being a human piñata for a wooly mammoth, it *is* pretty entertaining to watch other people's children hanging on for dear life in this crazy form of entertainment, available live in the great state of Texas. And did I mention that my new state can beat up your state?

A PROMISE

"When pride comes, then comes shame; but with the humble is wisdom" (Proverbs 11:2).

A PRAYER

Lord, I am so thankful that my child sometimes knows the limits of his capabilities. For him to say "pass" when encountering a risky situation makes this mother's heart burst with joy. Please help me to seek opportunities to teach my children that humility and wisdom often come hand in hand. I want them to know that it's okay to not always want to compete or be the best. Help me to teach them humility by modeling it in the way that I live.

Noise Noise Noise Noise!

A PERSPECTIVE

Eight-month-old Abby would not go back to sleep after I nursed her at six this morning. (Score one for Abby.) As a result, she was cranky sitting in the high chair during breakfast. When she's cranky the cute sounds of babble turn into the jabbering, nagging, nasal of an old crone. So during breakfast I endured a constant stream of:

BaBaBaBaBaBaBaBaBaBaBaBaBaNaNaNaNaNaNaNaNaNaNaNa MaMaMaMaMaMaMaMaMaMaAaaaaaaaaaaaWaWaWaWaWa

Naturally, after breakfast I tried putting her down for an early nap. But she cried the whole time she was in her bed. When I picked her up to rock her to sleep, she got a huge grin, looked around her room as if she had never seen such an interesting scene, and bounced herself up and down on my hip. Although I knew she was tired, I brought her downstairs to play while Isaac and I brushed our teeth. (Score two for Abby.)

She played well for a few minutes but as I was getting changed for my exercise walk, she began to fuss again. At the same time, Isaac began demanding attention. He started clamoring for me to give him one of my necklaces from my jewelry box. So now, the chorus was a discordant duet:

BaBaBaBaBaBaBaBaBaBaBaBaBNaNaNaNaNaNaNaNaNaNa
Mom, I want a necklace please. I want a necklace! I need help!
MaMaMaMaMaMaMaMaMaMaMaAaaaaaaaaaaaaWaWaWaWaWa
Mommy, open the doors! Can I have a necklace Mom, *please*?

As I was telling Isaac he did not *need* to wear one of my necklaces to go for a walk in the stroller, I made the mistake of saying the word "walk" out loud. Upon hearing her favorite word of all time, Bitsy realized that her most cherished outing was imminent. All morning the dog had been following me around staring at me with her piercing death-ray eyes, silently demanding her breakfast and her walk (and for heaven's sake some attention please!). Not able to contain her excitement any longer, Bitsy too joined the cacophonous chorus, adding her yap and her overzealous jumping to my over-loaded senses:

BaBaBaBaBaBaBaBaBaBaBaBaBNaNaNaNaNaNaNaNaNaNa
I want my robots in the stroller. Mom! Help me find them!
Yap Yap Boing Boing Yap Boing Boing Boing Yap Yap Boing
MaMaMaMaMaMaMaMaMaMaMaAaaaaaaaaaaaaWaWaWaWaWa
Find my robots Mom! I want my robots in the stroller, *please*!
Yap Yap Boing Boing Yap Boing Boing Boing Yap Yap Boing

At this point, all the noise was more than I could bear. I decided we didn't really have time for a walk *anyway* since we have to leave in an hour for Bible study and I still needed to get ready. So I took off my exercise clothes and hurled them at the dog to stop her yapping. It worked (and don't worry, no animals were actually harmed during the making of this story). Then I let Isaac watch a few minutes of television while I tried once more to put Abby in her bed. She refused to sleep *again*. Instead, she played mostly contentedly on the floor of the bathroom while Isaac bathed and I took a shower. (Score three for Abby.) Within half an hour we were all dressed and ready to go. Did Abby sleep during the twenty-minute car ride? Nope. So, she squawked her way through my Bible study discussion and forced my early departure. (Score four for Abby...does Mom ever get to score?)

Naturally the little imp fell asleep as soon as the car was in motion *this* time. She transitioned well from the car seat to her bed and stayed asleep just long enough for me to feed Isaac and myself a quick lunch, get him in bed, and start writing this entry. The kids' naps had *ten minutes* of overlap as Abby's ended and Isaac's began. That's ten minutes of...silence. Ten minutes of quiet, of peacefulness, soothing to my ears.

Abby's now sitting next to me on the bed, happily playing with some toys as Isaac finishes his nap and I decide how to conclude this entry. No, wait, she's caught sight of the laptop and is now trying to wiggle over here to pull off all the buttons and slam the screen closed. Naturally, I can't let her do that. "No-no Abby!"

BaBaBaBaBaBaBaBaBaBaBaBaBa...
(Score five for Abby. GAME OVER.)

A PROMISE

Praise Him with loud cymbals; Praise Him with clashing cymbals! Let everything that has breath praise the Lord. Praise the Lord! (Psalm 150:5-6).

A PRAYER

As You know Lord, in my house we make many *loud* and *clashing* noises. Frequently everything that has breath in our home is making sound. However, many of those sounds are not harmonious and far too few of them are in praise of You. Help me, God, not to simply add my voice to the often dissonant clatter of my household. Instead, help me to teach my children the joy of making a beautiful noise to You. Lead us to worship You even in the midst of our chaos!

Mom vs Man

A PERSPECTIVE

My husband makes a terrible mom. Don't get me wrong. He is a *great father*: he provides for his family responsibly, he balances his time well between work and home, and he plays with his kids. He's totally engaged in fatherhood. But as for his mothering skills, well, they stink (sorry dear).

For example, one sunny day I am preparing dinner in the kitchen while Isaac is enjoying a snack of baby carrots on the couch in the living room next to his father. Suddenly, from the other room, I hear the short, guttural sound of a child choking. As a mom, I know this sound by heart. With something like the "sixth sense," a mother has the ability to identify the sound of a child choking from miles away and respond appropriately while blindfolded and with one arm tied behind her back. But Isaac's *father*, who is sitting within inches of his son, does not notice the sound at all. I holler from across the room: "Hello? Child choking!" which engages Adel's paternal reflex of lifting the child's arms up over his head to open the wind pipe. Thus Isaac survives another case of fatherly attention.

On another day, Isaac is munching on a bowl full of nuts on the couch next to Adel, who is holding eight-month-old Abby. They are watching something on television and I go to my room to change my shirt before heading out for dinner (the encrusted snot clashes with my shoes). When I reenter the living room, five minutes later, the bowl of nuts is spilled all over the couch, Abby actually has two or three peanuts *in her mouth*, and Adel is sitting there obliviously staring at the TV set. Hello? Choking hazard! Possible peanut allergies! At the very least, an unnecessary mess!

Then there's the harmless daddy mishaps that occur on a regular basis. These are mistakes that a daddy seems far more prone to make than a mommy. More than once I've said, "Honey, for that outfit, the buttons are supposed to go up the *back*, not the *belly*." This one was especially comical in Isaac's little infant onsie that had a cute fuzzy bear face on the rump. Only when Adel put it on backward, the bear face was right at eye level with Isaac's...um..."manhood." Funny.

As a mom and dad, we are just wired so differently. It seems to me that my husband's philosophy is to let the children make their own mistakes so they can learn from them. That is a good point, of course, but let's brush it under the rug for a while. As a *mother* I would much rather avoid the hurt in the first place. Adel will let the child stand on a chair so that he'll know how it feels when he falls off. I would rather make him get down and tell him that he might get hurt. When Isaac does fall down and is crying on the floor, we react completely differently. I lift him up to comfort him while Adel walks past and says, "See, I told you to be careful." Wired *so* differently.

Regardless, while Adel and I don't always see eye to eye on these and other issues of safety and child-rearing, I have to admit that I don't have much room to complain. We're in this together. Adel respects what I do "for a living" as a real job. He works hard all day long and he knows that I do too. Once he comes home, we split the evening's chores evenly. We cook together and wash dishes together or at least trade off between cooking and keeping the children from poking each other in the eye.

But he does even more than just help with the evening's chores. He is actively learning to be the spiritual leader of our family, something I highly value. He backs up my discipline and doesn't tolerate or ignore it when our toddler disobeys or disrespects me. And he lets his children (and his wife) know daily that they are loved through his words and his time. He sends us the clear signal that he would rather be here with us than anywhere else in the world. See, his *mothering* skills may stink, but he's an awesome father (and husband!).

During our toughest time as parents, when Abby was a newborn and Isaac was having sleep issues, we would stagger downstairs together after finally getting both kids to sleep, plop on our bed, and give each other a look of exhausted triumph. We had made it through the day! Even though we're so different, there's something endearing about going through this time together.

A PROMISE

"The righteous man walks in his integrity; his children are blessed after him" (Proverbs 20:7).

A PRAYER

Lord, thank You for blessing me with a husband who truly loves me and understands my needs, as silly as they may seem. Thank You for continuing to grow him into a wonderful man of God and a father who is deeply involved in the lives of his children. I pray that You would grant him wisdom as we work together to make the best decisions we can for the lives of our children.

Potty Training 101

I had been skillfully avoiding the subject of potty training Isaac for quite some time. But finally, after subtle hint number four thousand twenty-three dropped gently but persistently by Mimi, I decided that I might as well at least give it a test run. After all, he was two-and-a-half and I thought it would be so nice if he could learn to use the potty regularly before Abby graduated from college.

So, I invited Mimi to come and help with a day of potty training (with nine-month-old Abby crying every time I had to run to the potty with Isaac, Mimi's help was invaluable!). Now, Dr. Phil claims he can potty train any child, no matter how stubborn, in a day. I would have been happy to let him test his skills on Isaac. But since he was not available, Mimi and I rolled up our sleeves to follow his instructions ourselves. As for Isaac's response to our efforts, he basically said (although not literally): "Potty training? Ha....potty train *this*!"

Here's how it went.

During naptime, Mimi and I prepared for the training session to begin. We got a stuffed bear and dressed it in one of Isaac's shirts and a diaper. When Isaac woke up from his nap, we had him help take off the bear's diaper and put on a new pair of "big boy undies." Then we gave the bear (and Isaac) lots to drink and set the bear on the little toddler potty. By hiding a water bottle under the bear's shirt, I was able to simulate the bear going "pee pee" so Isaac could watch. He was fascinated. Then we had a potty party for the bear, making a celebratory ruckus with the kids' play instruments. Finally, we put a stamp on the bear's hand and congratulated him on his success.

Isaac couldn't wait to have his own potty party. So we put him in his own pair of undies, gave him some chocolate milk, and waited. I was glad that I had the camera ready for a snapshot of my little boy prancing around in his first pair of underoos. There's nothing cuter than those string bean legs sticking out of a pair of sagging underpants.

Sure enough, in a few minutes, Isaac was wiggling uncomfortably. He did not want to wet his new undies. I took him to the potty, and gently wrestled him onto the seat. Despite his apparent potty phobia, he did finally sit there for about three seconds before he declared himself finished. The potty was dry and his bladder was full but we pulled up the undies, stamped the hand, and continued to wait.

A few minutes later the inevitable "oh no" expression crossed Isaac's face and a thin, pale stream trickled down his leg. I grabbed his hand and cheered excitedly as I led him to the potty. (By the way, it is *not* that easy to cheer and smile when your child has just sprinkled your carpet, but Dr Phil says it's a must, so cheer I did). Again Isaac begrudgingly sat on the potty with no results. His undies were only mildly wet, leading me to believe that there was more coming.

With growing excitement, we watched Isaac play and waited for the next opportunity. About one hour and one more lightly soiled pair of undies later, Isaac finally could hold it no longer. As luck would have it, this blessed event occurred right where we wanted it to: on the potty! (Since the first little tinkle accident we had been taking him to the potty every five minutes, just in case, so by this time his hands were lovingly pockmarked with a rainbow of stamps he had earned each time he sat down). This time, to Isaac's surprise when he stood up, the potty had a nice big puddle of pee pee. We gave him the honor of dumping it into the toilet and flushing. Then we had a great big potty party for Isaac.

One would think, and Dr. Phil might assert, that after such a success, victory would be inevitable. But one potty party seemed to be all Isaac needed and he quickly became uninterested in our game. Been there, done that. He also no longer esteemed his undies as something worthy of protection and he concluded the evening with two more thoroughly soaked pairs. It was at this point that I decided we needed waaaaaaaay more undies if we were going to do this right. I had six pairs and did a load of laundry half way through and we still needed more. At bedtime, we all breathed a sigh of relief as we put a clean dry diaper on Isaac and said goodnight. "Okay," Mimi bolstered, "that went okay. We'll try again in the morning!"

But the morning proved no different and I grew increasingly weary of the effort. By mid-morning, after Isaac had peed and pooed in his last pair of clean undies, we all agreed to put off the potty training for a few more months. Isaac clearly needed time to get more comfortable with the idea of sitting on a gaping hole and I needed to have my head screwed on better to pull it off. Until we were both more ready, I decided that I would continue to allow Isaac the blissful freedom of being able to pee and poo whenever and wherever the heck he pleases.

So this is going to be a process for us. Not, as some of my friends tell me, a simple task. I seriously know several people whose kids pretty much potty trained themselves. Not so with us. I for one will not be able to look back blissfully on potty training and say, "I just put my son in his underwear and threw away the diapers and he started going pee and poo in the potty right away. And now he's using his stock market investments to pay in advance for his PhD at Harvard and he just discovered a cure for cancer and has developed a plan for attaining world peace by next summer!!! Isn't that wonderful?!?!"

It can be hard sometimes not to compare. My niece, who's the same age as Isaac, was potty trained at eighteen months and here's Isaac a whole year later, and still in diapers. If I think about it that way, it can make me start to feel like a slacker-mom. Or worse, it can make me start to judge my own child in comparison with another. But comparison is a silly road and I know better than to journey there. It's much better to remind myself that each child has been created entirely uniquely. Besides, he may not have any interest in peeing in a potty, but you should see that boy run. He can run circles around his panty-wearing cousin any day! Entirely unique.

Actually, as much as it would be a nice boost for my ego to say potty training my child was a piece of cake, I don't really feel all that bad for how the attempt turned out. I just don't think Isaac was quite ready for it. Honestly, I don't think Isaac's *mommy* was quite ready for it either. I look forward to the day when I can look back on the task of potty training and smile, knowing it's completed. Until then, I will wait patiently (and with relief) for the right time to begin again.

A PROMISE

"To everything there is a season, a time for every purpose under heaven" (Ecclesiastes 3:1).

A PRAYER

Thank You Lord, for freeing me from unnecessary urgency. Thank You for allowing me to give myself and my children a break when we need it. I pray that You will grant me Your patience as well as the discernment to know when the season is right.

Making Friends

I have come to the conclusion that I'm at a point in my life when it's rather awkward to be making new friends. I really enjoy the mommy group I joined with Celeste, but after months of playdates and activities I still feel vaguely like a stranger in a room full of people.

For one thing, though I know nearly everyone's name in the group now (there's roughly thirty-five of us), and even most of the kids' names too, I really can't say I *know* many people in this group yet. But let's be honest, it's extremely difficult to build relationships with other women when the only conversations you have are when kids are running around everywhere.

Here's a typical mommy playgroup conversation:

Mommy #1: So, we just bought a new house. We're so excited!

Mommy #2: Oh, that's great! Where is it located?

Mommy #1: Just a minute, Johnny is dumping the flowerpot on Cathy's head! (*runs off to intervene*)

Mommy #3: (*joins conversation*) That's a cute shirt. Where'd you get it?

Mommy #2: It was on sale at Macy's. Oh, there's the snacks! Reagan, do you want a cracker? (*goes to help her child get a snack*)

Mommy #4: (*joins conversation*) Did you watch *American Idol* last night? It was so funny.

Mommy #3: No, I was so tired I went to bed. Hold on a second. Mandy just fell. (*runs off to comfort her child*)

Mommy #5: (*joins conversation*) So, what size diaper is little Kevin wearing now?

And so on. Typically, the mommies exchange a line or two, get interrupted by the antics or needs of their children, and then move on to start other one-liner conversations with the other mommies in the room. So, by the end of a playdate, we have all had roughly fifty meaningless and unmemorable conversations. One huge exception is, of course, the mommies who have only one, stationary infant. Those moms have the luxury of being able to sit together in little clumps and sustain conversation together. Sure, they're occasionally talking over the wails of their babies, but they're still *talking!*

When I'm at a playdate, I usually leave feeling so frazzled from keeping up with the activities and needs of my two little ones. Typically I feel the only memorable impression I have made on my potential new friends is the general sensation that some sort of spastic, winded tornado has just blown through the room. I'm pretty sure that once I drag my kids home, the conversation of the "mommies of single, stationary infants" (or MOSSI for short) goes something like this:

MOSSI #1: What was that?

MOSSI #2: Oh that was Megan. She has two children and she's pretty much a spastic, winded tornado.

MOSSI #1: Oh. Okay. So, what size diaper is little Kevin wearing now?

Okay, I'm being goofy. The mommies in my playgroup are wonderful and I know they forgive my frazzled nature. They also actually have more remarkable things to talk about than the size of their infants' diapers. But even though the other moms are interesting and kind, I am still finding this to be a challenging time to be making new friends.

My crazy, hormonal acne isn't helping my friend-making efforts, either. It's not that anyone else seems to mind it; it's just that it makes me feel so self-conscious. One morning, when my acne was especially horrendous, I took the kids to the library for story time, hoping to remain anonymous. Naturally, I bumped into Jennifer and Allison, two of the mommies from my group. Feeling heinously unattractive, and wishing I could crawl into a hole, I awkwardly approached them to say hello. They were kind enough to invite me to join them for lunch after story time.

A few minutes later I pulled my car into the parking lot of the pizza place where we had said we'd meet. As I walked toward the door, I felt nervous and insecure. I looked horrible and I knew I was really asking for trouble to try to have a meal with my kids *in public*. To top it all off, I then had the poor fortune at that very moment to exhibit an extreme episode of dorkiness.

Dorkiness, dear friends, is a genetic malady. I inherited mine from my parents. Boppa is a self-proclaimed goober. Those of us fortunate enough to know him closely are daily confounded that he is able to hold a high-ranking position at his place of employment, such

162

is the extent of his gooberness. Mimi, though she doesn't have the same, lovable, goober-quality of my father, frequently falls victim to the whims of Murphy's Law. My paraphrased version of this law is: anything bad that can happen, will...especially if it involves making you look like a dork. For example, for several consecutive years, Mimi was attacked by an annual Christmas zit. This zit landed regularly during Advent, right on the tip of her nose, calling to mind a striking resemblance to Rudolf. How festive! So, as you can clearly see, I have good reason for blaming my dorkiness on my parents.

On this particular day, as I opened the door to the restaurant, my own curse of dorkiness struck when a gnat flew right into my eye and refused to leave. Holding Abby on one hip, my diaper bag falling off my shoulder, and with one eye closed, I dragged Isaac past the table where Jennifer and Allison were setting up high chairs. Instead of stopping to talk or help set up, I led my disheveled crew straight to the bathroom to dig out the black speck that was floating around my cornea. In a few seconds I was better, although my eye was a bit red. Before heading back out to face my new friends, I took a moment to assess my sad reality. How much dorkier could I be? Not only was I queen of teenage zit-faced angst, but I also now had to go and explain to my new friends that the reason I just rushed past them to the bathroom was because I had to fish a bug out of my eye.

Naturally, they shrugged it off and welcomed me to the table. The next few minutes were a flurry of buckling high chairs, piling food on plates, and filling cups. I struggled to keep it together serving the two little ones and trying to feed myself. Between bites, spilled drinks, and intervening the cavorting of my children, I attempted a few conversations with the two ladies. Among topics, I was able to share with them about my current struggle to live each day with my children *joyfully*. It was good to be real and let them see a little piece of my heart. I walked away flustered as usual, but also feeling like the time had been well spent. We had made a little connection, built a little bridge, founded some fledgling friendships. It's a good start.

I find myself, in retrospect, wondering how different these past nine months would have been if my friendships were already in place *before* I had Abby. What if the women in my mommy group had known me when I was a calm, collected, clear-skinned mother of one? Okay, so I was rarely calm and collected even then (remember when I locked myself out of the house in the rain at eight months pregnant?). Still, the odds were stacked much more in my favor!

The reality is, as a new mommy of two, I could seriously have benefited from the support of an *already established* circle of friends. If nothing else, this whole experience has helped me understand the importance of friendships. We were not designed to journey this life alone and I now have a new motivation for helping others who find themselves similarly with too few hands for the tasks that need to be done. However, in spite of all that I seem to be working against (acne, genetic dorkiness, and a seriously flustered demeanor) I feel like I'm slowly, slowly, slowly making good friends in my new home.

A PROMISE

"Two are better than one, because they have a good reward for their labor. For if they fall, one will lift up his companion. But woe to him who is alone when he falls, for he has no one to help him up" (Ecclesiastes 4:9-10).

A PRAYER

God, I thank You for the dear friends I already have as well as the new friendships that grow stronger every day. I know that friendship, and the blessings that come with it, is a gift from You. Mostly Lord, I praise You for being with me even when I feel alone. I know that I can never be overcome as long as I can claim You for a friend and companion.

164

Boobs

If you're a guy and are squeamish about the subject of breastfeeding, you should probably not read this entry. In it, you will find controversial and alarming words such as *nursing, breast, elastiboob, boob job, buxom, heaving,* and *milk.* Come to think of it, what are you doing reading this book anyway? This is clearly a book for MOMS as the title suggests and if you are a guy I am a little doubtful that you have found a way to acquire this distinction. Nevertheless, consider yourself duly warned that this entry will be almost entirely about boobs.

Although breastfeeding is my preference, I have found that it offers unique challenges. As an infant, Abby wanted to nurse every two hours. When you factor in the amount of time it actually took to breastfeed, every two hours seemed more like every twelve minutes. This pattern greatly increased my odds of having to nurse in public. I am not one of those women who is overly comfortable with my own femininity enough to want to share the experience with total strangers. When I nurse, it requires stealth.

It was at this time that I attended the wedding-day festivities of my good friend Liz, for whom I was a matron of honor. Adel did a great job watching Abby for the duration of the ceremony. But even with his help, I still had to take a break every two hours and find a secluded room in the church. In the privacy of said secluded room, I would have to completely unzip and remove the top portion of my stiff, formal gown, allowing Abby to get to the goods. Although we were well tucked away, I still felt uncomfortably exposed, sitting topless while my husband stood guard. It was a *church* after all. Filled with (gasp!) *church people*! What if one of the deacons walked in, trying to figure out who left the lights on in the dressing room? *That* would have been awkward.

Only slightly less awkward than this is the experience of nursing a child on an airplane, where you hardly have enough room to cross your arms, much less lay a child down horizontally to nurse. The poor child must lay there with either her feet or head exposed to the on-coming traffic in the narrow aisle. Or if you happen to be sitting next to a well-dressed business traveler, it's, "Excuse me sir. Please pay no attention to the small feet dangling in your cereal bowl while I nurse my child."

When the baby gets older, there's the distraction factor that adds an extra challenge. Both my kids, at around eight months old, started becoming increasingly difficult to nurse. I could no longer nurse them in public. At the slightest sound, the nursing child would lift up his or her head and struggle to sit, convinced they were missing out on a live performance by Hannah Montana or at the very least, a speech by the president of the Elmo fan club.

My sister says her girls did this too, but the difference between us is in how our boobs respond to the sudden change of plans. My boobs, to put it frankly, are quite volatile. Once the milk starts flowing, it really shoots out at an alarming rate. If Abby starts to nurse and then stops to see what's going on in the room, she gets a face full of milk. She doesn't like this one bit and will start to cry, refusing to nurse *ever again* because of the traumatic and horrifying experience. It is because of this that I can only nurse the child in the quiet of a soundproof, padded room where she will not be distracted in the slightest bit.

Another challenge of breast feeding is initial breast-to-baby size ratio. When nursing a small newborn, the infant seems so fragile and the breast seems so gigantic and intimidating. You're afraid you might crush the little face when your enormous "boob in the sky" descends to offer sustenance. But a baby grows large at roughly the same rate as a mother's breasts become elastic. Soon, you can lay your baby on the couch in the living room and she can happily nurse upon your elastiboob while you prepare dinner in the kitchen, in some cases even if your kitchen happens to be in Madagascar and your living room couch is in Beaumont, Texas.

In spite of the troubles one can run into when nursing a baby, breastfeeding also has a great many benefits. My frugal husband favors it because it's free. My babies both preferred it to the bottle and quite simply refused to take a bottle after learning to nurse (stinkers). Doctors say breastfeeding is healthier for babies than formula. And nursing mothers claim a sentimental bond with the nursing child. Breastfeeding can be a very rewarding experience for all of these reasons, but for me, the greatest reward I've received from nursing is the "boob factor."

As a young woman, I was not endowed with a large, buxom, or "heaving" bosom. Throughout my teenage years my dearest friends and family honored me as the subject of the most heart-warming and solicitous humiliation. Some of my favorite catch phrases were "flat as a pancake," "flat as an ironing board," "size negative double D," and "if you were any flatter you would have inverse cones." Ah, those days were hilarious. I'm still laughing today.

Actually, I've even had the honor of my flatness drawing the attention of total strangers. When I was in college I served on a jury for six weeks. During a short break in the trial, one of my fellow jurors pointed out her ample, perky breasts and told me she had recently had a boob job. "You're so cute," she baited. "You really could use a boob job too." I'm pretty sure I walked away soon after scraping my lower jaw off the cement floor.

I spent years living with mortifyingly small breasts. This is why, for a flat-chested woman like me, the best part of nursing is that for the first time in my life (and without a boob job thank-you-very-much-Ms.-Jury-Lady) I have BOOBS!

I went to a baby shower for a friend of mine when Isaac was about two months old. Enjoying my newly abundant breasts, I wore a low cut shirt (which doubled in value for being high-waisted and thus hiding my still-flabby tummy). Somehow at that shower, I got to talking with another woman about boobs. I swear I was *not* the one to bring up the topic as it is a subject I have spent most of my life trying to *avoid*. The other woman was complaining that her boobs were too big. When I confided that I've always had the opposite problem, she exclaimed in surprise and told me that she thought I had the perfect breasts! I looked down doubtfully at my chest. Indeed, with the low-cut neckline and Isaac's feeding long over-due (he was at home putting up a fight with his daddy over the bottle) my breasts looked quite Hollywood. I can honestly say that was the *first* and *only* time anyone has ever complimented my boobs.

Okay so even with my traumatizing boob-less background, I have enough sense to admit that I can't keep breastfeeding forever just to keep my new, womanly figure. Actually, with Abby now at nine months old, I'm really beginning to look forward to the end of nursing. I'm excited to have my body back to myself. Of course, as Jennifer, a kindred small-breasted spirit, says, "The best thing about quitting breastfeeding is that you get your body back. The worst thing about quitting breastfeeding is that you get your body back." Yup. Bye-bye boobs.

And that, my dear friends, concludes this controversial and offensive entry on all things related to boobs. You can call your husbands and father-in-laws back into the room now. I promise it is safe again for the overly squeamish.

NURSING! BREASTMILK! BOOBS!

Gottcha. ;)

A PROMISE

"Your two breasts are like two fawns, twins of a gazelle, which feed among the lilies" (Song of Solomon 4:5).

A PRAYER

Lord, what is the big deal about breasts? You've even included creative descriptions of them in Your word! (And I'm pretty sure you weren't giggling when You did, either). Our culture views them as icons of womanhood and sexuality. If that's all there is to it, I'm afraid I come up flat. (What a pun.) But I am actually quite satisfied with the body You have given me. I thank You that it is through my imperfect body that You provide the gift of perfect nourishment for my babies. It amazes me that by Your design, an infant can thrive on mommy's milk alone.

Momma Said There'll Be Days Like This

A PERSPECTIVE

I had a rough morning, and for once I couldn't really blame it on my kids. There was nothing all that unusual about this morning. It was just an accumulation of ordinary mishaps. But, when added together, even commonplace events can result in an extraordinary experience (or an extraordinary headache).

It was after breakfast that things really got icky. In the garage, I saddled up the kids in the jogging stroller as Bitsy excitedly tugged on the leash. Just as I clicked the leash into place, I noticed the hair on her forehead was looking irregular, as if something was lurking just beneath the fur.

Sure enough it was a giant, revolting, engorged tick. In its fullness, it reminded me of a disgusting gray version of the girl who turns into a blueberry on *Willy Wonka and the Chocolate Factory*. A rudimentary tick inspection turned up about half a dozen or so other ticks, one of which was nearly as inflated as the first one. After trying in vain to get an emergency appointment with Bitsy's groomer, I decided we had more important things than exercise to do today.

I put ten-month-old Abby in her bed for a (hopefully) restful nap and I turned on Sesame Street for Isaac. Then I scooted Bitsy outside with her doggy shampoo and my tick-removing gear. This gear includes tweezers, a bowl half-filled with water to plunk the nasty creatures into, and a pair of medical gloves because heaven knows I am not going to willingly touch one of those repulsive insects. I bathed Bitsy and used the rinsing-off time to inspect beneath her thick, fuzzy undercoat. Having unearthed roughly a dozen new ticks in the process, I flushed all the pests down the toilet.

This unexpected event did not make for a good start to my day. And, to add to it, before I was even finished with Bitsy, the next round of fun began. I had brought Abby's monitor out with me while I bathed Bitsy so I could hear when Abby stopped playing around and finally fell asleep. She had been quiet for a few minutes when I heard a distinct "Moooommmmyyyy" coming through the speaker. *That can't be Abby*, I thought to myself. Sure enough, as the voice sounded again, I recognized Isaac calling for me through the monitor in his sister's room. Abby, probably having just been jarred awake by Isaac's close-quarter's yell, proceeded to cry passionately. I hurriedly finished up with Bitsy and then rushed upstairs to see what in the world was going on.

Nothing makes me more exasperated with Isaac than when he wakes up his sister. "What are you doing?" I hissed at him between clenched teeth. "I'm looking for my mommy," he replied innocently, seemingly unaware that he had caused any grief to anyone. "I want some fish water," he whined, referring to the fish-shaped cup I keep by the upstairs bathroom sink. Too annoyed to argue, I filled the cup, handed it to him, and told him to go downstairs after he was finished drinking unless he wanted a good spanking. He did as he was told, thank heavens.

Then I comforted Abby, replaced the dropped binky, snuggled her back in her blanket, and laid her down again for her nap. At this point, she had been in her bed for more than half an hour and, sleep or no sleep, she was tired of being there. So, my usually mild, uncomplaining Abby uncharacteristically cried as I closed the door. But she settled down after a few minutes and I could hear her tossing and turning again in her crib.

I rushed to shower since it was quickly approaching the time I was supposed to arrive at the strawberry farm where I had planned on meeting the ladies from my Bible study. During my shower, Abby began to cry and only intensified her protestations as the minutes ticked on. Finally, throwing on some clothes, I rushed upstairs and relieved her from her prison. She was instantly glad and played around my feet while I finished jamming our things into the diaper bag and loaded us into the car.

In my haste to help Abby, I had forgotten to put on a sanitary pad while getting dressed. I was at the end of my first period since being pregnant with Abby and out of practice with the ritual. Hurried and flustered, I did not even have the sense to notice that the pad was missing. Thus, I set the scene for the third, and final (thank goodness), mishap of my morning. Abby of course fell asleep *just* as I pulled into the parking lot of the strawberry farm. Leaving the car running, I pulled Isaac out before he woke her up and made me more frustrated.

I called the ladies from my small group as Isaac and I hovered outside the car. That's when I found out from Misty that there were no strawberries left at the farm. I don't mean that we had just arrived late in the day and all the ripe berries were scavenged already. In this case, we arrived late in the *season* and the entire berry field had been plowed, leaving not only no berries but also no plants. Just rows and rows of dirt. Does this sort of thing happen to anyone else, or is it just me? We had rushed through our hectic morning, sacrificed Abby's naptime, and stressed over being late...and all for rows and rows of dirt.

Great. So, the ladies and I stood outside the little fruit market with our kids playing at our feet while Abby napped for a few more minutes in the car just in front of where we stood. That's when I

172

noticed the feeling of ooze. This would not have upset me, having become accustomed to it over the last few days of my period, except for the fact that it drew my attention to the spot where my underwear meets the corner of my legs. It was that corner where I expected to feel the secure, puffy crinkle of a sanitary pad. Instead I felt only the thin, damp cotton of my underwear. Inwardly, I rolled my eyes at myself, playing the morning back in my head and realizing where I had gone wrong. Well, there was nothing for it now. I needed help, and quickly. I had to cast aside all my pride and any last pretense of being a together, with-it kind of gal.

"So," I addressed the ladies in the group, trying to talk over the heads of the curious preschoolers present. "I don't suppose any of you happen to have a feminine hygiene product with you?" Thank heavens, Christy, for reasons incomprehensible to the entire male contingent of our species, carries with her a small and varied arsenal of such handy disposable goods. I grabbed Isaac's hand and, leaving Abby (now awake) in Misty's arms, I went inside the market to ask where one could find the restroom in such a fine establishment as this.

As it turned out, in such a fine establishment, the only restrooms available were two port-a-potties located out back. Not really looking forward to sharing this experience with Isaac, but invested too far to turn back, I lugged him over to the scummy blue stalls. I selected one and was about to leave him outside the door to play with the pebbles. Then I realized how close we were to the driveway and thought that the few minutes of discomfort of having him in there with me would be worth the reduced risk of him being run over by a careless driver.

Ordering Isaac not to touch ANYTHING, I quickly locked the door behind us. Then, while he was looking into the murky depths of the unflushable toilet I took care of my most basic feminine hygiene needs. For once, Isaac was too disgusted to disobey my order *not to touch*. As we reentered the circle of our friends, he regaled them with a description of how the toilet did not flush. "White toilets flush," he informed them, referring to the ones we have at home.

What a fun, fun day, I thought to myself as we drove home. *I wonder what else lies in store for me?* But somehow, strangely, my kids actually saved the day for me once we got home. Abby warmed my heart when she rolled around on the air mattress in the playroom, laughing hysterically as Isaac bounced her up and down with the force of his jumping. Isaac made *me* laugh genuinely as he tried to retell the story of Dora saving Little Star but got too silly towards the end to use real words and started wiggling his tongue and murmuring goofy noises instead. Rather than causing me stress, the antics of my children actually melted away the gloom that had settled on my heart after this frustrating morning. That's a nice, unexpected, and welcomed turn of events that I hope to experience much more often. They are my precious treasures.

A PROMISE

"I have great confidence in you; I take great pride in you. I am greatly encouraged; in all our troubles my joy knows no bounds" (2 Corinthians 7:4 NIV).

A PRAYER

God, so many times I feel like my children are Thing One and Thing Two, especially when I focus on how much trouble they can cause! But I thank You for giving me a morning full of mishaps followed by a few lovely moments with my children to remind me (once again) how precious they are. Truly, in all my troubles, my joy knows no bounds!

It's Not Fair!

Parents can't help but treat the second child differently than the first. In some cases this actually works out in favor of the younger child, as in the case of the first child having to wait to drive until he turns eighteen while the second child is given the keys to the family car at age three. I really thought, based on my own experience as a second child, that I would work very hard to be fair with my own children. But I have learned that I'm pretty much slopping things up for my children just like all the other parents who have gone before me. I can just imagine my children moaning to their future psychiatrists:

Isaac to his psychiatrist: My mom didn't let me have a bite of her mall pretzel until I was over a year old. Not even a little bite! She was too afraid I'd choke. And I didn't get to eat sweets until my first birthday because mom was on some kind of wacko, wannabe-health-nut spree! But not with *Abby*...nooooooooo, *Abby* was given a whole soft pretzel all to herself to chew on when she was only six months old. Mom thought Abby was so cute gumming away at that thing. And Mom gave Abby sweets as early as she could chew! *It's...not...fair!*

175

Abby to her psychiatrist: Isaac is always complaining about the things mom let *me* do at an earlier age than she let him. But, while Mom was more laid back with me, she was also less focused on my every little accomplishment. With Isaac she would be like, "let's take a picture every two minutes just to be sure we don't miss anything that my little prince does...oh isn't he so smart!" Sick. With me it was different. As a newborn, people would ask her how many weeks old I was and she couldn't even remember! And you know, Mom still has Isaac's first-birthday picture as the wallpaper on her computer. I don't think she's ever going to change it, even though he's now thirty-five! *It's...not...fair!*

    I have to admit that it's all true. I'm completely unfair. I don't mean to be, it just happens! A perfect example is our treatment of Legos. Adel has been chomping at the bit for Isaac to play with his boyhood box of Legos pretty much since Isaac was born. I put it off until Isaac was two and a half years old for fear of the boy choking on those miniscule pieces. For a while, I upheld the policy that Isaac could only play with Legos when Abby wasn't around so that she too would be kept safe from the choke hazard. But before long, I realized that the policy took way too much effort and I decided to simply teach Abby not to put the Legos in her mouth (I know, fat chance!). By now the girl has been playing with Legos for longer than she can recall. I know, Isaac, it's just not fair!

    But, while the first child tends to suffer from a mother's over-protectiveness and attempts at perfectionism, a younger child can fall victim to a mother's lack of unabashed enthusiasm. By the time the second child is born, the mother has already seen and experienced much of the world of babyhood. There is little new under the sun for a second time mother. Each little milestone, each baby step, while still noticed and adored by the mother, is simply greeted with far less worship and idolatry than it was with the first child. Dave Barry, in his book *Babies and Other Hazards of Sex*, demonstrates this inequality through the parents' efforts toward each child's baby album:

> Baby albums are probably the single biggest cause of violent death in America today. The reason is that when people have their first baby, they record everything that happens:
>
> *January 5 - Today Rupert is exactly one and a half weeks old! He weighs 8 pounds, 3.587 ounces, up 2.342 ounces from yesterday! He had two poopy-diapers today, but definitely not as runny as the ones he had January 3! Also not quite so greenish!*
>
> And so on. By the time these people have their *second* baby, they're sick of albums. Oh, they try to slap something together, but it's obvious that their hearts aren't really in it:
>
> *1966-74 - Byron was born and is now in the second grade.*
>
> So Byron grows up, seemingly normal on the outside, but knowing on the inside that he has this pathetic scrawny album while his brother's looks like the Manhattan telephone directory, and eventually he runs amok in a dentist's office with a Thompson submachine gun. So if you want to do a baby album, fine, go ahead, but have the common decency to notify the police first. (154)

Being the "understanding" and "fair" parent that I am, I vow, in a lame effort to bridge the equality gap I've made between my children, to spend the remainder of today applying some "quick fixes" to the problem. I'm sure this attempt will do nothing whatsoever to make either child feel better but I have to at least try, right? I'll work

177

very hard today to allow Isaac to do something "dangerous" and uninhibited; something that any parent would balk at allowing for a first child but would easily ignore for a second child, having seen the first child live through it countless times; something like eating the dog's kibbles or standing on the sofa. I promise, I won't say a word. Live it up, buddy!

And for Abby, I realize I've written a whole lot lately about her older brother and not much about her. To make up for it, I'll spend the next five minutes writing a detailed description of how stinkin' special she is, just so she knows I actually did notice. Perhaps this written evidence of my adoration will balance out the fact that in nearly every photo I have taken of her, big brother is constantly jumping in front of the camera, yelling "Look at me, Mommy!" Here's Abby in a nutshell at ten-and-a-half-months old:

Beautiful

She has no ankles or wrists because they've been swallowed up by her chubby, cherubic, dumpling rolls. She has six teeth which she's had since about six months old. After that point, she just stopped growing teeth for a while and started growing eyelashes. It's not that she didn't have eyelashes before, it's just that they're growing in so long and thick now. That, combined with her full, cupid-bow lips and her smooth, bronze skin, has Adel out researching shotguns so he'll be ready when the boys start comin' 'round.

Strong

Abby's diaper changes have become genuine Greco-Roman wrestling matches, including the nudity (at least on *her* part!). I want her to lie on her back. She wants to crawl away. Therein lies the problem. So, while I'll be using one hand to hold both her ankles in the air, she arches her back and torques her shoulders, spinning around onto her belly in spite of my best efforts to wipe her bottom before poop gets smeared everywhere.

178

Sweet

At bedtime, Abby buries her head in her blanket, pulling its soft folds up to her face. Similarly, when someone talks to her, she pretends to be shy and snuggles her face into the crook of my neck with a bashful smile. She makes you want to say "awwwww" at least a dozen times a day.

Smart

She has quite the growing vocabulary for one so young, including: uh-oh, momma, da-da, tan-tou (thank you), more, bye-bye, ball, and Isa (Isaac). (Abby, don't tell your brother, but you picked up language much quicker than he did!)

And Isaac, here's some dog food and a wooden cork gun. Go crazy, kid!

There. That ought to even things out for a while.

A PROMISE

"Fathers [Mothers too!], do not provoke your children, lest they become discouraged" (Colossians 3:21).

A PRAYER

God, as a learning parent, I'm discovering it's really difficult to be "fair" all the time. It's just one more opportunity for "mommy guilt!" But when I step back and look at how You have made each of my children so preciously unique, I feel it's no wonder I don't treat them exactly the same. They're not the same person! Please help me to care for them both and build them both up uniquely but equally (lest they become discouraged!).

Two's Company

Two's company. And not very polite company either! They demand that their every whim be met instantaneously. They never pick up after themselves. And they seem to go out of their way to scatter their various playthings and edibles across every once-clean surface in my home. All this "company" sure is a lot of work!

Now, at almost eleven months post-Abby, I'm relieved to find that I have been more able to view raising my children as a fun adventure instead of one big, never-ending chore. I have an energetic and demanding boy who amazes me daily with his sponge-like ability to retain new information. I have a darling button of a girl who likes nothing better than to follow me around babbling *mina-mina-mina-mina* or *bida-bida-bida-bida*. I am beginning to see more of the rainbow through the clouds.

And I look forward to it getting even better. Soon Abby will turn one and enter that transitional year that somehow ends in a non-baby entity: a walking, talking person. I feel an enormous sense of relief that she's getting close to this goal. I have almost made it! Soon I'll have two toddlers. I can stop nursing. I can stop worrying so much about every little piece of lint that Abby might try to eat off the ground. And maybe (please, God!) things will get a bit easier to manage for me, having two in the same stage of the game.

On the other hand, there is a small part of me that pangs at the thought of never getting to nestle Abby's infant head to my breast or squeeze her pudgy thigh once she grows independent, lanky, and long. She is actually getting close to the age Isaac was when I got pregnant the second time. Naturally, these factors, against my better judgment, cause me to ponder the question of whether I want to have more children.

Are you planning to have more children? It's a question I've been asked a million times, usually by bystanders watching in amusement as I swoop Abby up with one arm, balance the diaper bag on my head, and use my other arm to elastically nab Isaac before he runs gleefully into the street. People want to know just how nutty a mom actually can be. And though my answer varies widely, depending on my mood, it is usually, "No way!" As much as I like things to go my way (control freak), I must admit that it's a very good thing God, and not me, is really in control of determining how my family will turn out. My problem is that, unlike God, *I* keep changing my mind! What follows here is a brief history of my family planning policy changes:

Growing up, my sister Lindsay and I always imagined ourselves duplicating the happy scenario exemplified by our mom and her sister. Lindsay would have two girls, like our mother, and I would have two boys, following in Aunt Teri's footsteps. Lindsay's two girls and my two boys would be the best of friends, running brown-skinned down the beach, laughing up their soda pops, and spurring each other on to creativity and nonsense. That was "The Plan" –two boys for me and two girls for Lindsay. No doubt. No deviation.

Then I met the Kellys.

The Kellys were a lovely, picturesque family of six at the time I became acquainted with them. They had four angelic girls under the age of five. One week in college, the Kelly family accompanied our college group on a weeklong retreat. During that week, the girls flitted and blushed behind the legs of their parents, smiling sweetly and whispering darling observations to one another. Watching them splash about in the water or kick at small rocks with their little white sandals caused a stirring of maternal longing within me. They were Alcott's *Little Women* reborn. So I thought to myself, *maybe I really want girls and not boys. Maybe I want four girls instead. My own little women. Awww.*

Then I had Isaac. We were back on track with The Plan. Boys it would be for me! And with the pacing, and the rocking, and the singing, and the painful nursing, and the endless efforts to comfort an infant bent on crying for no reason, two would seem to be plenty, *if* we made it past the first one.

While Isaac was still swaddled and wiggly, I watched *Finding Neverland. Now that's what I need,* I thought to myself. *Four delightfully mischievous boys, each one cuter than the next and all with charming British accents! Why shouldn't I have a houseful of boys running amuck, who would no doubt adore me as their beautiful and selfless mother?* (No need for the peanut gallery here...this is *my* fantasy). So I decided that I would not necessarily call it quits after baby number two. I would at least leave my options open.

But while Abby's due date quickly drew near, Isaac showed more promise of turning into a real life Tigger (you know —"bouncy, trouncy, flouncy, pouncy" and "jumpy, bumpy, clumpy, thumpy" and "Fun! Fun! Fun! Fun! Fun!") than of turning into a real-life British gentleman. At that point, I was pretty sure I would call it quits at two. I was still a little bit in denial that the baby in my belly was a girl though. That wasn't The Plan at all!

When Abby was born, I immediately thanked God that *His* plans are not changed by the whims of emotions and the pressures of circumstances. He had a gift planned for me in my beautiful girl and it didn't matter how much I tried to plan my own way (thank heavens!). As I look back over this history of my changing opinions, I am humbled to admit that perhaps I should be turning to God for His guidance. God knows my family and my circumstances. He has a plan for us. Although I'm not yet certain whether His plan involves extending our family of four, I trust that He will guide us and get us where we need to be.

As it turns out, Lindsay also deviated from The Plan by getting pregnant again with a third! And her first two are only fifteen months apart! *How's she going to do it?* I think. *Poor fool.* Right now I feel like I could never handle a third child. Experience has taught me that with each additional child my chance of surviving intact greatly decreases. I find it impossible to fully meet the needs of each of the kids I already have (Come on, Mom, *all* we want is 100% of your attention, 100% of the time!). So until God nudges otherwise, this type-A momma is plenty content with her two kids. But Lindsay's not like me. She is flexible, relaxed, selfless (of course, she'll argue with that last statement, but, whatever, it's true). She feels no need for white-knuckle control over her circumstances. She'll be fine with three.

And for me, these days, when I see a pregnant woman in passing, my emotions swirl. True, there's a twinge of jealousy at the beauty and mystery of the experience, but mostly there's a healthy dose of pity. *Poor thing*, I muse. *I hope she knows what she's in for!* And then, with less pity and more self indulgence: *Better her than me!* And with that, I wrestle my two children into formation and schlep on home.

A PROMISE

"A man's heart plans his way, but the Lord directs his steps" (Proverbs 16:9).

183

A PRAYER

    Lord, motherhood is such a rollercoaster of a journey that I find my opinion changes rapidly in regard to my ideal number of children. Right now I feel that I cannot possibly handle any more children. These two are more than a handful already. But I admit that Your plan for my life is better than my scheming. Guide my decisions and mold my heart to be like Your heart, and my thoughts to be like Your thoughts.

Potty Training 201

A PERSPECTIVE

Isaac's second round of potty training occurred over two months after the first failed attempt. We went to Mimi's house to maximize the "helping hands" and the timing worked out nicely as we were also waiting for my sister to have her third baby at a nearby clinic. This time we were more prepared: I brought with me at least thirty pairs of "big boy undies" for Isaac to go through in a day if necessary, we had a potty seat in nearly every bathroom in the house, Isaac had been practicing sitting on the potty for the past two months so he was no longer deathly afraid of it, and Mimi had bribe central set up and ready to go.

As for the *bribes*, er, I mean *incentives...rewards?...*what PC term are we using these days? Who cares! As for the *bribes*, *I* was going to use the old stamp-the-hand trick but *Mimi*, ah good ole Mimi, pulled out the big guns before we even got started:

Mommy: Isaac, if you go pee pee on the potty, do you know what you'll get?

Isaac: I don't know.

Mommy: (*opening her mouth to say, "a hand stamp!!!" with great enthusiasm*)

Mimi: (*interrupting*) You'll get a candy!!! And if you go poo poo on the potty, you'll get a present!!!

Isaac: Hooray!

Mommy: (aside) Uh Mimi? I hope you're the one providing the presents!

So, with our "total bribery" system in place we set about accomplishing round two of potty training. My plan was to take Isaac to the potty at the first sign of wiggling. Since the child wiggles constantly anyway, we visited the potty roughly 8,923 times that first day. He had a few accidents, but managed to hit the target on most attempts. It was surprisingly easy this time!

We also managed to get him to do his first ever poo poo in the potty that morning. I know, from changing Isaac diapers for the past 2.75 years, that he tends to "purge the works" just after breakfast. So, as soon as he swallowed his last bite of pancake, I sat him on the potty and brought in about twenty books we could read while we waited. Mimi helped by making sure Abby didn't lick the wall sockets while my back was turned. On about book number three, Isaac made his poo-poo-in-the-potty debut. Of course, his first words after this momentous occasion were, "Mimi, I need my present!"

After several days of this intense bribery, and with Isaac doing so well, I told him that from now on he would get only jelly beans for a poop deposit and nothing for going pee in the potty. His mater-of-fact reply was, "Jelly beans for pee pee. Presents for poo poo. That's the rules." You can't pull the wool over *his* eyes. Despite Isaac's shrewd bargaining skills, we were able to curb the gift giving and scale back to jelly beans for a number two and nothing but a heartfelt "good job" for a number one.

After a while, he actually grew quite fond of his own bodily functions. Often he would hop off the toilet, announcing, "Look what I made!" He would examine the poo in the toilet before exclaiming it to be "huge" or "just one little nugget." And once, after plopping a series of tiny "little nuggets" into the toilet bowl, he put on his cutesy voice, "Awww, look at the little babies!" Then he leaned over and blew air kisses at them. I laughed and then told him we don't kiss poopoos.

So for some time, everything seemed to be going great with potty training. That is, until Isaac experienced his first public restroom toilet. This particular toilet had an automatic flush that went off with a tremendous ROAR while the poor child was still sitting on it. He sprang up like a monkey and wrapped his arms and legs around my legs like a tree trunk, screaming hysterically.

Since that day, Isaac has nurtured quite a phobia of the larger, noisier toilets found in public restrooms. (Although I have learned the nifty trick of putting toilet paper over the automatic flush sensor so that he never gets a surprise like that again!) As a result of his public-restroom fears, I purchased a handy dandy foldable potty seat that I can carry with us wherever we go. For the most part, it's pretty useless. Now, instead of Isaac yelling, "No, no, no! I don't want to," from the seat of a public toilet, he's yelling it from the loftier perch of his foldable potty seat, sitting atop the public toilet. Oh well, at least he's doing great at home. And I have this great new excuse to carry an even bigger-than-ever diaper bag to accommodate the new portable potty seat!

I just keep reminding myself, "One day it will click." It's just like our first attempt at potty training when we both were simply not ready for it. It would have been foolish of me to force it before its time. Now I have to function under the same hope that I had back then, that one day he'll have it all mastered and I don't need to worry too much or push too hard to make it happen in my timing. I can only hope he'll "get it" before he takes the neighbor's daughter to the homecoming dance.

A PROMISE

"The end of a thing is better than its beginning; the patient in spirit is better than the proud in spirit" (Ecclesiastes 7:8).

A PRAYER

Lord, I am so thankful that You have used this experience to teach me to be patient instead of proud. Pride, along with pressure for my child to keep up with his peers, can sometimes lead this mommy to try to force an abrupt ending to every milestone. I am an impatient person by nature, and I know You are teaching me through our recent success (and failures) that patience and wisdom work much better than pride and will-power!

FWD: Happy Mother's Day!!!

A PERSPECTIVE

Lindsay and I are the worst daughters ever! For Mother's Day this year, we did *nothing*. Okay that's not completely true. We did go out to lunch with Mimi the day before Mother's Day, but I'm not sure if it counts since Mimi paid. After lunch, Mimi took us shopping and bought a cart full of toys for *our* kids. Then we went back to Mimi's house where the guys, who had been watching the kids for us, were waiting with grilled steaks. After dinner, Boppa gave all three of us gals a fancy box of chocolates and we spent the rest of the evening taking bites of each one to find the ultimate best piece of candy in the box (it was the chocolate mint).

You would think that once we had children of our own and understood how much our mom did (and still does) for us, once we understood her constant sacrifices and her beyond-human efforts on our behalf, that we would appreciate her enough to plan ahead. Lindsay has a pretty good excuse considering that her baby, over a week past its due date, is probably preparing to make its big debut any second now. My only excuse is that I have none. So I tell my mom "Happy Mother's Day" and make jokes about what a lousy daughter I

189

am while seriously appreciating the royal treatment from *my own* mom and dad (what a schmuck!).

I also enjoyed receiving a gamut of Mother's Day emails lovingly forwarded by friends and family who must all be pregnant because why else would they be so emotionally sensitive as to willingly forward one of those emails? You know what I'm referring to here—those sappy email forwards that we all get and open and read, even though we know they are going to be sappy. They go something like:

> *"To every mother who has ever wiped a child's tear,*
> *To every mother who has ever lovingly*
> *put a bandage on a boo-boo,*
> *To every mother who has ever held a precious newborn,*
> *To every mother who has ever kissed a tender brow,*
> *To every mother who is sentimental enough to actually read this nonsense:*
> *She must forward this to twelve other mothers by next Tuesday to avoid*
> *being cursed for life by the email fairies who will slowly pull out all her hair*
> *and force her to listen to "Air Supply's Greatest Hits" over and over*
> *again.*
> *Happy Mother's Day!!!!!!!"*

The worst part is that sometimes those email forwards actually bring tears to my eyes. And sometimes, when my mind becomes completely possessed by forces from far beyond the realm of cheesiness, I actually forward them on to new victims. Well, as sweet and heart-warming as those Mother's Day forwards can be, I have a bit of a grudge against them because I have not found them to be at all a realistic portrayal of motherhood. Sure, motherhood is the best gift ever! But these emails tend to portray motherhood with a rose-colored bias.   Where's the drudgery?   Where's the snot and the poop? Where's the thankless, unheeded hours of repetitious nagging?

I have decided that it is time to stop complaining about it and start my own Mother's Day tradition to correct the situation.   So I composed the Mother's Day forward for the realist. This is <u>real</u> <u>life!</u> (These events have either happened to me or to someone I know.) I'm talking bodily-function extravaganza, slogging-through-the-endless minutes, crazy-out-of-control motherhood.

A Mother's Day Forward for REAL Moms:

- To every mother who has ever gotten up with the baby at 2:02AM…and 2:16AM…and 2:39AM…and 3:24AM…and 4:31AM…and…,
- To every mother who never crosses her kitchen floor without tripping over a misplaced toy or crunching a Cheerio underfoot,
- To every mother who has ever caught throw up in her hand,
- To every mother who can't understand why the child who refuses to eat vegetables will daily eat nasty things off the ground like cigarette butts, dried worms, previously chewed candy, and dog poop,
- To every mother who has been forced to say a fond farewell to her girlish figure,
- To every mother who knows that a thick crust formed just under the child's nose actually prevents the snot from flowing and saves a lot of tissue,
- To every mother who has learned (the hard way) that children never grow out of needing back-up clothing on outings,
- To every mother who counts down the minutes until naptime, and then bedtime, and then naptime, and then bedtime…,
- To every mother who has ever reached the point where it doesn't bother her that the kids eat the food that's fallen on the

kitchen floor (even though she swore she would never be *that* kind of mother),

- To every mother who has ever been locked out of the house by a toddler who has just learned to turn the door latch,
- To every mother who has ever turned around for one minute during bath time and looked back to see the small child finger painting the bathtub with her own poo,
- To every mother who has locked her keys in the car...with the child in it...and had crowds of people gather to gawk and cluck their tongues at her as police cars and fire trucks rolled in to "rescue" the trapped child,
- To every mother who has questioned the validity of making the bed if it's just going to be slept in a few hours later,
- To every mother who has ever been peed on...in public,
- To every mother who has witnessed her breasts inflate, then stretch, then shrink, then sag,
- To every mother who never once dreamed as a young girl that she would become so enthralled with another person's bodily functions,
- To every mother who has been forced to use a public toilet while holding a baby on her lap because she forgot the stroller and really, *really* had to go,
- To every mother who has ever sworn she will dismember that toy (you know which one I'm talking about) if she has to hear that annoying song one more time,
- To every mother who knows that a child never gets dangerously ill during doctor's business hours,
- To every mother who has ever had to wash poop off the big-boy undies, *and* the shorts, *and* the child's legs, *and* the potty seat, *and* the floor,
- To every mother who has given up on keeping the dog toys out of the kid's mouth and the kid toys out of the dog's mouth,

- To every mother who has ever felt that five o'clock just can't get here fast enough,
- To every mother who spends countless hours reminding the toddler to say "please" and "thank you" to no avail and then is flabbergasted when that same child repeats an "adult-vocabulary-word slip-up" after hearing it only *once*,
- To every mother who would drop dead from sheer joy if just once someone would thank her for all the seemingly insignificant things she does,
- To every mother who knows that no matter how many pacifiers she owns, she will only ever be able to find *one* (if she's lucky!),
- To all you mothers out there who know what it's <u>really</u> like to be a mother and love it anyway,

May your ceaseless efforts be rewarded with a child who grows into a person of righteousness and wisdom, causing you to rejoice!

Happy Mother's Day!

A PROMISE

"The father of the righteous will greatly rejoice, and he who begets a wise child will delight in him. Let your father and your mother be glad, and let her who bore you rejoice" (Proverbs 23:24-25).

A PRAYER

Lord, this job is tough. I spend a lot of time engaged in utterly thankless tasks that no one but me seems to even notice. In the end, I want my children to know me, not as the woman who patiently cleaned the smeared poop off the floor, but as the mother who raised them with integrity and grace. I pray that my children will grow into godly people who will make me proud to be called their mother.

The Waiting Game

A PERSPECTIVE

Lindsay was seven days past due with her third baby when I headed with both kids up to Mimi and Boppa's house to await the new arrival (just before Mother's Day). Her first two babies were each eleven days late so we naturally expected that she would have this baby on or before (preferably) the eleventh day. Either way, I figured I wouldn't have too long to wait. And, let's face it, Mimi and Boppa's house is always a fun place to be because I can forget for a while about all the chores that aren't getting done at my own house. Besides, it was almost the weekend and I had wanted help potty training Isaac. All the stars were aligned for a good, long visit to Mimi and Boppa's house. I just didn't know how long!

On day number ten past her due date, we started to believe that Lindsay's baby would never come. Her midwife confirmed our suspicion: "You're dilated to one and your cervix is still nice and thick." Just what every expectant mother wants to hear at ten days past her due date! I pressed the issue further, wanting cold, hard facts, and asked if the baby was likely to arrive in the next twenty-four hours. "Not likely," was the reply. So with that grim news, we went back to Mimi's house to "wait" who knows how much longer for this mysterious baby to arrive. *No sense in going home at this point,* I thought. *I've already been here for three days, what's a few more?*

While we waited, we played a kind of waiting game with the older children. Lindsay, unconventionally aggravating as she is, likes to keep the gender of the baby a secret. So we spent far too much time discussing whether we would get an Elias or an Amelia:

Lindsay to her daughter, Lily: Is mommy going to have a boy or a girl?

Lily: A boy!

Lindsay: What should we name him?

Lily: Pink!

Lindsay: That's a very creative name.

Megan to Isaac: What do you think is in Aunt Lindsay's tummy?

Isaac: Food!

Megan: Actually, there's a baby in there.

Isaac: A baby dinosaur!

Megan: No, a baby person. Do you think it will be a boy or a girl?

Isaac: A boy.

Megan: What will his name be?

Isaac: Oscar!

Megan: That's a good name. Lily thinks it's going to be a boy named Pink.

Isaac: It's a baby dinosaur! It come out and say "boo!" It say "roar!"

And so it went, day after day, until finally we truly believed that the baby would remain inside her belly forever. On the thirteenth day past her due date, we had pretty much given up on ever meeting our new family member. Then Lindsay had an ultrasound appointment to check on the health of the all-too comfortable baby. We were shocked to received a phone call informing us that she was actually going to be induced right there on the spot because her fluids were low. We were all completely flabbergasted and rushed around like a bunch of crazies, as if we had not had thirteen days of waiting to prepare for this moment.

Now, Lindsay likes to experience natural childbirth. At least, she must like it because she had done it successfully two times before and planned to make this a third. But when the contractions get strong and painful she needs a team to help her get through. So, upon receiving the phone call of her imminent delivery, we all frantically fumbled about to prepare for our assigned roles.

At the hospital, we were informed that, with the threat of being induced, my medicine-wary sister had actually gone into natural, voluntary labor. Now why didn't we just threaten her sooner? Good question. If she ever decides to have a fourth child, I will begin one week prior to her due date to make anonymous midnight phone calls threatening to induce her if she doesn't go into labor soon. But for this baby, it was far too late for that and the game was afoot.

The beginning of someone else's labor is actually quite boring (I guess I *sort of* understand now why Adel fell asleep during my early labor pains with Isaac). It seems to me that labor loves to strike at night, just when you're ready to curl up with a good book. So Mom, Andy, and I spent the first few hours watching *Signs* on the hospital

196

television and ruthlessly eating our dinners in front of Lindsay while she sat through the early, minor contractions, obediently following the hospital policy of fasting during labor.

As for the "labor team" assignments, I am the designated "lower-back-pain-counter-pressure-masseuse-and-comic-relief-through-downright-absurdity-and-childish-antics person." This is a very important job and I take it very seriously. So, *after* I finished my leisurely dinner and a movie, I decided to be enthusiastic about getting to work. Knowing that my sister is notorious for dragging out her labors for a full twenty-four hours, I persuaded her to do ridiculous squats with me up and down the empty maternity hallway while Mom and Andy laughed at us from behind. Lindsay kept it up until her legs were shaking and she decided it was time to rest.

The nurse checked her a bit later and announced that our efforts had moved Lindsay from a "one" to a whopping "two." Immediately after the exam, during which the nurse had intentionally tried to stimulate labor, Lindsay started to experience truly painful, intense contractions. This hopeful sign was enough to help me convince Lindsay that one more trek around the hallways ought to do it. So off we went, squatting during contractions, me applying lower-back pressure to help with the pain and Lindsay breathing through the contraction. At the next check, an hour or so later, Lindsay had progressed to six or seven centimeters and was clearly in the throes of labor. Andy's job kicked in at this point as the "support-and-encouragement guy." Mimi sat back a while longer, anxiously awaiting her job as "mopper-of-the-brow-with-the-cool,-damp-cloth lady."

When the sweat started beading and Mimi started mopping, we called Lindsay's midwife. She arrived just before Lindsay was ready to push to be the "giver-of-instructions-and-conveyer-of-general-confidence-in-Lindsay's-capability-to-deliver-this-baby-without-an-ounce-of-pain-medication person." With the nurse bustling about as we all did our jobs without fail, Lindsay pushed out a tiny baby girl just five minutes before the doctor arrived (yes, the same doctor who will remain unnamed and infamous for threatening the induction and being the "instigator-of-Lindsay's-unplanned-labor-at-the-hospital-instead-of-at-the-midwife's-clinic-where-she-had-done-all-her-prenatal-checkups-and-was-hoping-to-deliver-in-a-natural-environment-that-would-avoid-the-bureaucracy-and-red-tape-of-the-hospital-setting-not-to-mention-avoiding-those-ridiculously-high-medical-bills doctor"). At least we all had the satisfaction of having the baby already delivered and healthy by the time the doctor walked in to do his "important" and "scientific" job.

So, fourteen days late (since she was actually born at 1:30AM the day after Lindsay's labor started), Amelia Leigh came into the world. It certainly wasn't our timing! It also wasn't according to plan the way that she was born in the hospital, instead of the midwife's clinic. But God often seems to function outside of our best laid plans. And what a blessing it is when His plans fall into perfect balance. In God's great timing, little Amelia has arrived to delight her two older sisters and disappoint her one older boy cousin on this side of the family who was desperately wishing that Aunt Lindsay would give birth to a baby dinosaur.

A PROMISE
"This is the day the Lord has made; we will rejoice and be glad in it" (Psalm 118:24).

A PRAYER
Thank You, Lord, that Your timing is perfect! We don't always understand the way things turn out. But in something as miraculous as the birth of a baby, the details and expectations often pale in comparison to the miracle and joy of new life. We rejoice in this perfect day!

The Silver Lining

I've never heard anybody say that parenting is easy. If someone was audacious enough to do so, parents in the near vicinity would probably start throwing tomatoes at them (or Cheerios, which can easily be found in the nearest diaper bag). As a stay-at-home mother, I find that most days and moments are lovely. And then there are days and moments that I half wish I could delete from the record, Big Brother-style. Some of these moments are just plain ugly. I'm not talking dirty-diaper ugly. I'm talking momma-losing-her-mind ugly.

Lately, it seems like Isaac and I have been having way too many of those ugly moments. Tension between us occurs so frequently these days that Adel calls it our "shining" (as in Jack-Nicholson-snaps-and-tries-to-annihilate-his-entire-family shining). If Adel comes home from work and tension is thick in the air, he'll say something like, "I see your shining is in full force today." Never mind that it probably doesn't speak highly of my maturity that I am easily reduced to squabbling with a two-and-a-half year old! And I'm sure my clever son is just playing his mother like a tired, predictable violin solo, but knowing that does not help me respond to his tantrums with patience. Nor does it help me focus on the silver lining instead of just the clouds.

I want to tell you about our day today. It is a perfect example of the ugliness I'm talking about because the "shining" occurred twice, in its full and hideous glory. Now, my son is a two year old. It is normal to expect some ugliness coming from him in the form of temper tantrums and such (and oh, let me tell you, ladies, he knows how to work it!). However, things don't *really* get ugly until The Momma starts losing her patience.

Our day today started out as one of those lovely ones. During Abby's morning nap, I had given Isaac a ride on a pillow, calling it "Aladdin's magic carpet." He loved it. It was one of those special moments to savor for a lifetime. But that happy scene is not the one that has played out over and over again in my mind. Sadly, what I remember most about today is overshadowing friction.

This afternoon, as we were heading upstairs for naps, Isaac spied the "magic carpet" pillow again. He instantly demanded a pillow ride right then and there. It was not, "May I have another magic carpet ride, Momma?" Or even, "Carpet ride please!" No no, my friends! My son has a flair for drama like his momma, and since it was just before naptime, his emotions were threadbare. So his demand came in the form of a near-tears whine: "Carpet ride! Carpet ride! Carpet ride!"

Under different circumstances, I would have corrected his demand into a polite request and then taken him on the pillow ride. But in this case, my arms were overloaded already and it had been a long morning. I tried to reason with him: "How can I carry Abby, the sippy cup, your two blankets, *and* you on a pillow? I need both hands to carry you on the magic carpet pillow. Let's do it after naptime instead." He threw himself down and kicked and screamed.

I realize that this is normal toddler behavior. And I should have responded with patience and reason. But my emotions were also threadbare, because, let's face it, I get tired too. I gave him an ineffective warning and then swatted his bottom and dragged him up the stairs, while poor Abby struggled to breathe in the death-grip of my other arm. A more resilient momma would have been able to shrug it off and enjoy the rest of the day. Instead, I found myself irrationally irritated, saying regretful things that I never should have said: "Why can't you just obey? Why do you have to be so selfish?" It makes me so sad that a moment like that is what resonates in my mind instead of the charming moment we had earlier of a child's gleeful laughter and a mother's playful attention.

Our second conflict occurred at bedtime. After a frustrating poo-accident, I was looking forward to some pleasant moments of quiet relating over bedtime stories and prayers. I felt we needed another lovely exchange to rectify this trying day. I told Isaac to pick a book to read. "Two!" he said. "Okay two," I agreed, in the familiar and universal ritual of bargaining over bedtime books. We both usually enjoy this one-on-one time. I snuggled him onto my lap and read *The Rainbow Goblins* and a library book on astronauts. Then I said, "Okay, it's time to read your daily devotional." He freaked out. A writhing, shrieking, arms-flailing freak out.

"No! I want my Bible!" he shouted, pushing away from me in an attempt to force his way to the picture Bible that lay on my other side. (Okay, as I'm writing this it does seem pretty comical that one of our greatest power struggles of the day was over whether to read his devotional or his Bible! But it is what it is. Maybe it's a sign that I'm doing *something* right?)

I waited (patiently this time) until he stopped shouting enough for us to talk about our differing opinions. Then he settled down and, with prompting, restated his demand in a slightly more humble tone, "I want to read my Bible *please*." I told him we could read his Bible, but only *one* story. He agreed to those terms and I let him choose the story he wanted to read. He chose a *thrilling* old-testament story about Joshua and Caleb trying unsuccessfully to convince the fearful Israelites to enter the land of Canaan. Lots of talking; not so much action. Sounds like a riot, right? Yeah, Isaac didn't think so either.

201

When I finished reading, he had a complete meltdown. A writhing, shrieking, arms-flailing meltdown. "I don't like that story! I want another story!" he screamed over and over again. Now, I can understand his frustration. He had been hoping for more of the slaying of giants, or loading animals into the ark, or even Jesus walking on water, not a bunch of people sitting around talking. I actually felt a bit sorry for him and considered relenting for a moment. But, given his recent history of demand-making and his completely out-of-control, writhing, shrieking, arms-flailing behavior, I felt it best to stand my ground. I replied, as calmly as I could, "I'm sorry you didn't like that story. Maybe next time you can choose a different story. But we're finished reading for tonight." This statement was met with a full five minutes of back-arching wails. Not wanting to send him to bed on such terms, I waited and talked to him, offering a compromise by putting the disputed Bible in his bed so he could "read" it himself if he wanted to.

Finally he was calm enough for our bedtime prayer. Tonight my prayer was not sing-song or rote. Tonight it was heartfelt and earnest: "Lord, please help us not to fight so much. Please help Isaac learn to use his words instead of just screaming and please help Mommy to be more patient with him. Help Isaac sleep well so he feels better in the morning."

After that we snuggled as I sang him a bedtime song. I tried so hard to conjure up good feelings but I mostly felt sad. I was sad that we have been battling so much lately. I was sad that my memory of today will be clouded with our tension. I was sad because sometimes loving him means that I can't let him have his way even though he fights so fiercely to win. I long for us to unceasingly resemble that idyllic family portrait on our wall: the four of us snuggling together, smiling, playing happily, mutually respectful, harmoniously frozen in time. But my reality doesn't seem to want to fall in line sometimes and it can leave me disheartened. And when I am disheartened, I tend to focus on the negatives.

However, upon reflection, I think I can see a silver lining to this cloudy subject. Though I don't always respond to Isaac' tantrums the way I want to, I sometimes *do* get it right. That's a good thing. And when I mess up, God meets me with forgiveness. That's a good thing. With His forgiveness, I can even learn to forgive myself. That's a good thing. Getting to know my mommy friends, I'm learning that I'm really not alone in this. That's a good thing. On the morning after a bad day, there's a brand new opportunity to get things right. That's a good thing. I love my son, no matter what. That's a good thing. And, somehow, he loves me no matter what too. That's a pretty darn good thing!

A PROMISE

"Finally, brethren, whatever things are true, whatever things are noble, whatever things are just, whatever things are pure, whatever things are lovely, whatever things are of good report, if there is any virtue and if there is anything praiseworthy—meditate on these things" (Philippians 4:8).

A PRAYER

Lord, there are so many aspects of parenting that are true, noble, just, pure, lovely, of good report, virtuous, and worthy of praise! Help me to remember and mediate on those beautiful moments while still dealing responsibly and patiently with the unsavory ones. Thank You, thank You for the lovely moments!

Apples and Oranges

A PERSPECTIVE
Both of my children are adorable and sweet…yada, yada, yada. Still, it is impossible not to compare them to each other, especially since they are so obviously different. It's amazing how early you can spot the personality of a child.

On the night we brought Isaac home from the hospital, we were nervous and unprepared for what was to come. At night he was awake for hours at a time, mostly crying, and we walked with him up and down the hallway of our little home for what seemed an unbearable eternity.

On the night Abby came home from the hospital, she slept, woke up to eat, slept, woke up to eat, and then slept. Period. There was no pacing the hall. There was no stress or frustration over lack of sleep. There was no inconsolable baby.

When Isaac was an infant, the church nursery actually recruited a wonderful old man we called "Grandpa" to come be Isaac's pal because our son required one-on-one attention (seriously!). From the window of the room where I met to have Bible study with other women, I would often see Grandpa pushing Isaac around in a stroller. The report I would get upon my return was usually, "Well, Isaac did okay today but he was kind of fussy until grandpa took him out in the stroller." And every mom knows "kind of fussy" is nursery-worker lingo for "screaming his head off."

When I pick up Abby from the church nursery they always say, "Oh, she was so good today." She usually sits in the swing sleeping or quietly observing the commotion around her. Once, she was so quiet the whole time that they nearly forgot she was there. I'm pretty sure Isaac's caregivers never have that problem!

Isaac needs constant attention. Abby is happy just being near the action. Every time I walk past her as she plays quietly on the floor, I feel I must say, "Abby, behave," as if she needs my advice. Isaac is intense and Abby is mild. Isaac eats the peel, and Abby eats the peeled fruit. Isaac licks the frosting and Abby eats the cupcake. They are so different and yet I love them both the same.

Here's a chart that depicts the differences between an unidentified, but actual, pair of siblings*:

	Child #1	Child #2
Sleeping	As an infant, he cries all night and naps sporadically during the day. Even as a toddler, when he wakes up he instantly screams and cries until his mother comes to get him.	As an infant, she sleeps all night and most of the day. When she wakes up, she plays quietly in her crib, sometimes examining the fuzz balls on her blanket for the better part of an hour, before raising a fuss to be picked up.
Eating	Even as a baby, he will not, under any circumstances, allow the mother to feed him with a spoon. Instead, he insists on smearing every food item around his face and hair **all by himself!**	She eats most of what is offered and willingly allows her mother to feed her with a spoon like a normal child should.

205

	Child #1	Child #2
Playing	As a baby, he insists on being held by his mother **at all times**. He will play happily on the floor for maybe a nanosecond before whining to be held. As a toddler, he demands constant and undivided attention from his mother.	As a baby, she plays happily on the floor with toys and whatnot, only requiring her mother's attention when she finds herself in a dangerous situation (such as halfway up the stairs).
Social Skills	As a baby, he scowls at strangers who greet him. As a toddler, he is more than a trifle aggressive when it comes to sharing toys. If anyone other than mommy is so bold as to attempt to show affection, he will revolt in a most theatrical way.	As a baby, she sits quietly watching the world go by, gently cooing or smiling at others in the room. She is happy to be held by anyone in all the world. Her philosophy is: attention is attention is attention.
Talking	His first word is "no" and his favorite word as a toddler is "mine." Once he really learns to talk, he never stops, repeatedly over-stimulating his mother's eardrums and causing her brain to periodically explode.	She easily learns conversational words such as "uh-oh," "mama," "dada," "hi," and "more" before she turns eleven months old. She uses her words for good and cuteness, not for evil and destruction.
Point of View	He initially regards everything with suspicion, sure that it is going to cause him irreparable damage. As a baby, in new situations, his motto is "cry first, ask questions later." As a toddler, he slowly begins to recognize patterns and gain some trust (the bathtub didn't hurt me the first 1,348 times I went in, maybe it won't hurt me this time).	She is initially trusting and open-hearted, assuming everything is as soft and gentle and sweet as she is. Her reaction to new situations is quiet observation or giddy excitement. She takes life as it comes, with mellow contentment.

This chart illustrates quite accurately how two children, born of the same parents, can be so different. Through the uniqueness of each child, God's handiwork becomes abundantly clear. These are not accidents, formed purely through the calculations of science or the whim of chance. These children are carefully crafted treasures, completely distinct and utterly unmatched in all the world. Even my scowling boy, whom God created to be skeptical and distant to all but his chosen few, to which he clings like an eternally hungry parasite...even this boy was designed with a divine purpose. These are God's masterpiece. These are God's handiwork. God has a plan for them and I am overjoyed to be a witness to their singular journeys.

A PROMISE

"For You formed my inward parts; You covered me in my mother's womb. I will praise You, for I am fearfully and wonderfully made; Marvelous are Your works, And that my soul knows very well. My frame was not hidden from You, when I was made in secret, and skillfully wrought in the lowest parts of the earth. Your eyes saw my substance, being yet unformed. And in Your book they all were written, the days fashioned for me, when as yet there were none of them" (Psalm 139:13-16).

A PRAYER

I praise you Lord, for the uniqueness of Your creation, that two children from the same two parents are still such complete individuals, wholly of themselves. Thank You Lord, that my children, though both so different from each other, are the same in that they are loved equally and passionately by You!

*These children and situations are real, but the names have been hidden to protect the innocent. And, no, this chart is not about *my* children! As if I would ever so callously compare one to the other! Never mind the coincidence that the chart describes a toddler boy and an infant girl. Just never you mind.

The Vet

A PERSPECTIVE

Today I survived a mildly disastrous attempt to take Bitsy for a routine veterinary checkup, accompanied of course by my *darling* children. For this fiasco of a morning, I *could* blame the vet for keeping us waiting nearly an hour. What children can possibly behave for that long in a room the size of a large public restroom stall? But the real blame for the morning's events lies with me. I should have left my kids with a friend (any friend!) rather than try to attempt such an appointment with them in tow. Mothers of the world! Now hear this! Even if you just moved to town yesterday and the closest you have to a "friend' is the neighbor you met thirteen hours ago, if you *have* to do anything that requires patience and your undivided attention, leave your kids with someone else!

I, however, was not smart enough to do this. So, eleven-month-old Abby sat in the stroller for an hour. Even this perfectly delightful baby has her limits. She would periodically protest her captivity, causing her binky to fall to the ground. Not sure how sanitary that ground is. Probably *not very*. But we'll hope for the best since I, more than once, dusted it off on my shirt and returned it to her mouth. Desperate times call for desperate measures, my friends!

For Isaac's entertainment during this office visit, I brought his handheld DVD player that plays the same episode of *The Wiggles* over and over again. That kept him busy for, oh, about ten minutes. Then he spent the remainder of the time asking if we could leave (263 times), going through the contents of the diaper bag, and turning on and off the light. When the vet finally condescended to see us, Isaac was at his wit's end and used my distraction to do all the things I had been telling him *not* to do for the past hour.

I stood trying to listen to the vet as she advised me on how to care for my dog. I occasionally caught a word or two she said (some useful bit of information that I could really take home with me such as "dog" or "pet" or "you"). But rather than attentively listening, in reality I was taking peripheral notes on Isaac's antics. First he unzipped my wallet and spread my cash and credit cards all over the floor. Then, he started digging through my purse. All the while my brain was actually having a detailed conversation with itself. Something like, "I wonder if I can pummel the child without the vet noticing? I don't know, but as soon as she turns around, he's done for. And is it getting hot in here or is it just me?"

As I nodded vaguely in the general direction of the veterinarian's monologue, I soon became aware that Isaac had sidled into position behind me. I felt a gentle tugging on the seat of my pants. At the time, I figured he was playing with my pocket or trying to coax me into a hasty exit from an excruciatingly boring situation. However, one quick glance behind me informed me of an entirely different story. What I discovered upon turning to look at my son was that he was drawing...on my rear...with my lipstick. Oh, *and* it was all over the bench too. How could all this happen in just one minute?

The vet, oblivious of my complete distraction and lack of mental capacity, continued to courteously cite lists of preventatives and general canine health care. In a flash, I plunked Isaac down on the lipstick-smeared bench, threatening death or worse if he moved, and pretended to take notes on a torn piece of paper I had pulled from a brochure on the wall. After a few more minutes I made it out of there with a pounding headache and what was left of my dignity.

As for the lipstick on my pants, I keep forgetting to check my rear in the mirror, and I have been walking around for several hours now, completely unmindful of the fact that I may have "rose blush pink" accenting the seat of my navy jeans. Classy. At least I was able to drop Bitsy off at the groomers there, where they informed me they could take her but wouldn't be able to bathe her until later in the day. Gee, that's too bad. I'll just have to wait until after Adel comes home. Then I can leave the kids with him while I kill some time at the shoe store before finally picking up the dog.

But before I go gallivanting child-free off to the shoe store, would somebody *please* remind me to change my pants? And, before I go off to my next appointment of any kind that will require patience and my undivided attention, will somebody please, please, *please* remind me to leave the kids with a friend? I keep forgetting that I am not condemned to "do it all" on my own. And sometimes it would be better for everyone involved if I didn't try to!

A PROMISE

"Bear one another's burdens, and so fulfill the law of Christ" (Galatians 6:2).

A PRAYER

Lord, this family would function a lot better if this momma would remember to share the burden every once in a while! Please help me remember to ask for help and allow others to help me. And please help me make and grow friendships with other mothers who would benefit from mutual support.

Finding my Brain, Finally!

Before children, a good book was my solace in the evenings. Reading would enable me to unwind and release the excitements and anxieties of the day. But after having children, I found it quite impossible to read a novel. My mind simply couldn't handle the extra pressure. To carry a complicated plotline in my head day after day; to remember details, names, places and descriptions; or to get lost in the experiences of the protagonists: those things seemed far too overwhelming and monumental for the scatter-brained woman whose head hit my pillow every evening.

Thus, after Abby's birth, instead of reading myself to sleep, I began to search for alternative methods of unwinding. Eventually, I settled upon...um...Spider Solitaire. Embarrassing though it may be to admit to this, for quite some time I was entirely dependent for sleep upon that stupid computer card game. I could not fall asleep without it. Really. To fall asleep, all I had to do was beat the game and *ahhhh*, lights out! The unusual nature of this addiction has prompted me to ponder long and hard as to why it was so appealing. After much analysis, I've figured it out and it all boils down to one word: *order*.

After Abby's birth, and when Isaac was at the peak of his terrible-twos mania, I hit a long season of feeling utterly out of control. In this season, all my efforts to keep order in my home seemed continually unraveled. I went to bed knowing that my to-do list would still be just as long as it was the day before, that I accomplished nothing that day for the betterment of mankind, and that the next day I would get to wake up to the cries of a child and do it all again.

During this season, I appreciated *anything* that could make me feel a little sense of control and order. I needed something I could win (and organize!) without using too much of my precious and hard-to-come-by brain power! And for heaven's sake, please let me complete something that won't be undone the instant my back is turned. This is why, when I solved that silly computer game, when I played my cards right, when I accomplished eight neat little stacks of cards, ace to king, I knew that at least *something* was right, neat and tidy, in this crazy world. Then, and only then, could I roll over, turn out the light, and fall asleep.

This ritual went on for some time (exactly how much time, I will not disclose in an effort to retain *some* dignity). But after a while I began to feel that the silliness had gone on for too long. My baby was growing, things were slowly getting easier, and yet here I was *still* playing that idiot computer card game night after night. It was time for a change. I was ready to engage my brain again in the world of literature. But how to begin?

I decided to use my returning desire for literature to also help deepen the friendships I had made in the mommy playgroup. After a series of book-related discussions on the online message board, I offered to host a "book exchange" event. It was to be an evening meeting *without kids* (hoorah!). Just some dessert, coffee, and a chance to discuss and trade favorite books!

On the evening of the book exchange about eight women showed up to talk literature and trade books. It was so different from the usual "kid talk" of our playdates that I felt intellectually engaged for the first time since becoming a mother of two. That night I began the slow road to discovering (once again) that I actually do possess a brain. This is a great feeling for one who has been playing Spider Solitaire for longer than she cares to admit.

What made the experience even more rewarding were the great conversations between the mommies, at playdates or other activities, which were fueled by sharing common literature. We are slowly rediscovering our collective dormant intellect that has been hibernating all this time behind conversations about diaper rash and double strollers. I am finding I even appreciate the opposing viewpoints over which books are "good." Our differing opinions cause me to stretch my own preconceptions and pick up books I would not have otherwise considered.

After some months, the book exchange has become a regular event on our mommy group calendar. The host changes, we have some regular and some occasional attendees, and the desserts vary as much as the hosts. But three things stay the same at every book exchange meeting: there are women, there are books, and there are women talking about books! Welcome back, brain.

A PROMISE

"The heart of the prudent acquires knowledge, and the ear of the wise seeks knowledge" (Proverbs 18:15).

A PRAYER

Lord, after a long break, I am back to exercising the brain You have given me! It is such a blessing to be able to stretch my intellect and share a common interest with a group of fun women. Thank You for providing outlets for connections beyond the usual "mommy talk." I pray that You will continue to provide opportunities to deepen and strengthen my mind as well as my friendships.

Baby Number Three!

Ha ha! You probably read this title and thought I was announcing an unexpected pregnancy! Well, sorry to disappoint, but that is not the case. This entry is devoted to an "educational" and "enlightening" comparison (based on one person's anecdotal evidence) of the differences between having two young children and having three young children.

I recently got to visit Lindsay and her girls. It was the first time I had seen little Amelia since I attended her birth two-and-a-half weeks prior. This visit gave me the chance to ask my sister a question I've been dying to know the *real* answer to: is it true that adding a third child is not that much harder than having two? I have heard this from numerous people, all of whom have three or more children themselves, and I have always regarded it with suspicion. I feel like these parents are trying to trick me into joining their insane faction of mass-market parenting. "Why buy two when you can buy three for triple the price?" However, I trust Lindsay, seeing as how we survived our childhood and adolescent years in each other's company and came out the other side still willing to claim each other as family. I know she will tell me the whole truth.

So I asked her: is it *really* not that much harder having three than having two? I fully expected her to say, "No way. Three is much crazier!" But she just smiled her serene, contented, Lindsay-smile and told me it's actually pretty true. She explained it so well that I now actually believe it (at least a little bit). Here's the gist of what she said:

When you have your first baby, you undergo a huge change. Before the child entered your life, you were only accustomed to looking out for yourself, meeting your own needs. With the addition of that first baby to your life, you have to adjust to meeting the constant demands of someone else. Everything comes second to his need to sleep, eat, play, and be clean. It takes a while to become accustomed to waking up at his whim or letting your food get cold so you can feed him first. But eventually, you learn to make this new baby-centered existence work for you. Cold food is still food and five hours of sleep is still sleep, so life goes on.

Then you have a *second* child and everything changes dramatically again. When you had only one child, there was very little reason for the child to cry since you were usually able to meet his needs in a timely manner. But with a second child to care for, it is impossible to meet everyone's needs instantaneously. So, as a mother of two, you become accustomed to a certain level of chaos that, as a mother of one, you did not even know existed. Sometimes one of your children will just have to wait for her needs to be met. Sometimes a child is just going to have to sit and cry because you can't get to him for a few minutes. You learn to prioritize, to find and fix the *squeakiest* wheel before it gnaws your ears off. You become accustomed to noise, to impatient children, and to multitasking at a whole new level.

Then, according to Lindsay, when you have a *third* baby, the transition is really not that much different. You are *already* accustomed to a certain level of chaos from your first two children. By then you have accepted that your mode of operation *is* chaos. It's true

216

that the new child adds a *new element* to this chaos, but it is still chaos. And chaos is what mothers of more than one child do best (not that we're good at handling it, but we sure seem good at attracting it!).

The transition is also made easier by the mother being able to treat the older children as a *unit*. By then, the mother has already learned to survive one baby and one kid. After the third birth, she has one baby and *kids*. And, if she's lucky, the *kids'* needs are mostly the same (as far as eating, sleeping, bathing, playing...). This is what makes the adjustment to the third child relatively smoother than the adjustment to the first or second child.

This explanation actually makes sense to me. For the first time, I really think I can understand why people say having three kids really isn't that much harder than having two. **_HOWEVER_**, (and I can't emphasize this enough) it does *not* convince me to dive into generating more children! You see, now that I am at the very end of my first year with two kids, I am beginning to move away, ever so slowly, from the initial chaos to which I have become accustomed. At some point (soon, please God?), my kids will actually be old enough to play *on their own* for an *extended period of time*!!! This year has been quite a whirlwind. I am ready for the calm after the storm.

But even as I write this, I remember how God wants to have a say in all of my family planning. While it is good to do research (something I perhaps should have done before having children in the first place!), ultimately I know that I need to bring my plans to God. I want to let Him be my guide and ask Him for His wisdom as I make important decisions that will affect the future of my family.

A PROMISE

"Listen to counsel and receive instruction, that you may be wise in your latter days" (Proverbs 19:20).

A PRAYER

Lord, I pray for wisdom as a parent, to make the best choices for me and for my children. As I think about the pros and cons of having another child, I pray that You would guide my heart and my mind. Thank You for surrounding me with wise people who can help me sort out truth from fiction as I make my way through this task of raising my children and planning my family.

Godzilla vs Mothra

As the title of this entry portends, my kids do not always get along swimmingly. They are siblings, after all. Their interaction has changed as steadily as Abby has grown through all the phases of babyhood:

Abby: newborn

When pregnant with Abby, I spent months building Isaac's anticipation of his new sister's arrival. And when we brought her home for the first time, he was keenly interested. But after those initial, brief moments passed, Isaac has since come to ignore Abby. As far as he is concerned, she is far less interesting than he imagined she would be and he can't understand why all the grown ups are always making such a fuss over her. She sleeps nearly all the time: in the car, in the bouncy seat, in the bassinet, in the swing. And when she's not sleeping, she just sits there looking around, not really focusing on anything in particular. Pretty boring for a toddler.

Abby: sitting up

Abby adores her brother. She is quite star struck when he is near. Who earns the most intense giggle fits from Abby? None other than big-brother Isaac. She coos and babbles with pleasure when he kisses her or holds her hand in a rare, tender moment. To her, he is a rock star! She lives vicariously through him, like a couch potato watching television. He's the celebrity she observes all day long. When he comes up to her face, she smiles as if she's saying, "*Wow*, he noticed me!"

In contrast to Abby's infatuation, Isaac, for the most part, continues to ignore his little sister's existence. He plays around her as if she's not even there while she watches his every move. Other than the occasional moments of affection, the only other interaction he has with his baby sister is when he wants to wrestle. Isaac takes great pleasure in rolling over, tackling, pushing down, and tickling his little sister. To my surprise, she almost always loves it. To put it in perspective, it would be like being bumped into at the grocery store by Brad Pitt. Sure, I'd be a little annoyed at the impact but it wouldn't take long before I was giggling and blushing too.

Abby: crawling

Things have changed around here! This stage of sibling interaction is entitled, "Mothra Versus Godzilla." In this one-act play, Mothra flits about over the city which has been meticulously and lovingly constructed by her older brother, Godzilla. With wisp-like grace, her pudgy fingers grasp innocently onto the tunnel of a railway track. Then she crushes the tunnel, spilling stiff Lego bodies left and right. She throws the remains into a nearby tower, bringing it and its inhabitants crashing to the ground. She may be a delicate moth, but she's a monster after all.

In slow-motion reaction to his sister's destruction, Godzilla breathes a veil of fire and flashes his glowing eyes before bellowing a most hideous dragon roar meant to scare the offending Mothra and get the attention of mothers halfway around the world.

In short, Isaac is no longer able to ignore the presence of his little sister. I am currently working on equipping him to handle this new interaction:

The *how to give away a few items from a hoard of dozens* strategy:
As Abby approaches the hoard, Isaac screams, "Abby, noooooooooo!" Mom intervenes: "Isaac, you have a whole box full of blocks, let's pick one or two to share with Abby." After threats, consequences, and eight million repetitions, this strategy is beginning to stick (but not without prompting).

The *you can walk and she can't, so why don't you move somewhere else?* strategy:
If the toy in question is something that Isaac is especially interested or invested in, this strategy usually works after the initial "Abby, noooooooooo!" Upon prompting, he will usually move a few feet to the right or left and have at least thirty seconds of uninterrupted play before Abby catches up with him. If he were a bit smarter, he would move to the next galaxy. That should be far enough to keep little sister out of his business.

The *how to enlist the help of a grown up* strategy:
I am trying to teach him that after he says "No thank you Abby," if she doesn't stop, he can ask for help. Then it's my job to move her away and distract her. So here's how it goes now:

Abby: (*eagerly approaching the Legos*) More, more, more!

Isaac: Abby noooooooooo!

Mommy: (*could easily intervene here but is too lazy and likes the teaching opportunity*) Tell her "no thank you."

Abby: (*clutching and tossing any unguarded legos*) Bita-bita!

Isaac: (*in escalating whine*) No thank you Abby. No thank you Abby! No thank you!!!

Abby: (*reaching for Isaac's Lego "project"*) Mina-mina-mina!

Isaac: (*desperately grabbing her hand*) No, Abby, nooooooooo!

Mommy: If she doesn't stop, you can ask for help.

Isaac: Help. HELP!!!

Mommy: (*finally intervenes and removes the offending baby sister, finger-sweeping three tooth-sized Legos out of baby's mouth*)

Scene repeats approximately ten times every hour.

Abby: walking

  With Abby's birthday coming up, this phase is right around the corner. She has already taken a few tentative steps. Will a walking little sister make things better or worse for big brother? From what I hear, it doesn't get any better for about eighteen years! I am just hoping, that with persistence and patience (two things I often run short of), I will be able to teach my children to...

A PROMISE

...“Do all things without complaining and disputing, that you may become blameless and harmless, children of God without fault in the midst of a crooked and perverse generation, among whom you shine as lights in the world” (Philippians 2:14-15).

A PRAYER

Lord, I ask for Your guidance as we experience relational “growing pains,” adjusting to the changes in interaction that come with individual growth. I ask that You would mature me as a mother and as Your child. Please grant me persistence and patience so that I can be a better guide to my children in all the phases and stages of childhood.

And Then There's the Blues

In the months after having Abby, I was not at all surprised when I experienced "the baby blues." It's one of those side effects of motherhood that we're told to expect. But more recently, I have learned that there's *the blues* and then, there's *THE BLUES*. As we moseyed on toward Abby's first birthday, I expected *all* the gloomy feelings to go away. After all, they're called "the baby blues" not "the toddler blues!" Instead, I found myself experiencing randomly-occurring bouts of minor depression, usually during those vulnerable afternoon hours. In the hopes that someone who reads this may be able to benefit from it, I'd like to share some of my gloomy day journalings (and the optimistic outlook that followed).

October Journal Entry | Abby: 4 months old

I'm beginning to notice a pattern in my days and I've come to the conclusion that I'm actually experiencing "baby blues." I never did with Isaac, which is ironic because Abby is a waaaaay easier baby! Lately, when the afternoon rolls around, it feels like this one day has already dragged on for a week and I'm sure the next couple hours before Adel gets home will seem more like three weeks. The clock seems to stand still and I can't shake the dark, murky feeling of melancholy that hangs on my shoulders like a heavy shroud. And even when Adel is home, it's not that much better because we have to somehow fix dinner and manage both kids until we crash and start the whole thing again. Depressing.

While I am making some effort to recreate a fulfilling life for myself as a mother of two, I have been slow to pick up the pace of my former, mother-of-one self. Any outing with the kids is so exhausting, it feels hardly worth it. And yet, staying home all day makes me feel isolated and dreary. And what's the first thing to get thrown to the wind when life gets tough? Daily time with God! How ironic that I'm so willing to chuck the very thing that would most sustain me during tough times. Perhaps I should be turning to God instead of chocolate to meet my spiritual needs?

Yes, Obviously.

No wait, I can't.

Honestly, there's not much room for debate here.

Give up my chocolate? *Pray* instead of *gorge*? Seriously?
Seriously.

Uh, God, I'm going to need a little help here…

Well, at least that's a start!

April Journal Entry | Abby: 9 months old

When I got dressed today I put on my army-green pants. They're way too tight, leaving my belly to ooze over the waist-line. But today I didn't care that my stomach was still flabby from leftover baby fat. Then I picked out my black t-shirt with earthy green elephants marching across the chest. The shirt usually just sits in my closet because it is way too short, a holdover from the 1990's when short shirts were "in." With the advent of my own personal muffin top, I really appreciate today's shirt style that extends well past the belly bulge and safely comes to rest at the hips. But today I didn't care that the shirt is out of style. More than that, I *wanted* to be out of style today. I purposefully selected this shirt because it makes me feel, in my own pathetic way, that I'm making a bold statement about my independence from the opinions and constraints of others. "Ha!" my clothing screamed to the world. "I can look bad if I want to!"

To enhance this rebellious whim, I elected to go sans makeup even though my face is freckled with last week's pimple scars. And I topped off my earthy ensemble with my silver dangle elephant earrings (everyone should own at least one pair of silver dangle elephant earrings, just in case) and the black onyx ring I made in a high school jewelry class. I always feel rebellious when I wear this ring; it must contain the spirit of my teenage self.

Let's just say this was not the look I would have chosen if trying to make a good first impression or to strike people with how "together" or "with it" I was. But that's just it: I was *not* trying today. I felt so tired of trying. I guess in a way, I was trying *not to* try.

After I got dressed, I flaked on the mommy group event that I said I'd attend. I really didn't feel like seeing people I know. It wasn't so much that I didn't want to let my new friends see me dressed as the elephant lady. It was more that I didn't feel like talking, and sharing, and *trying* to connect. I just wanted to be anonymous. So after a slow morning, I took the kids on a quick trip to the library for story time, just to break up the morning. Then it was back home for lunch and nap time.

And now, here I am, writing about my attitude problem and trying to figure out why I am feeling so tired of *trying*. Maybe the mythical "Supermom" has really gotten to my head! Maybe I'm just frustrated because I've been unsuccessfully chasing after her apron strings, trying to catch up to her lofty standards! It's like I'm smart enough to know Supermom doesn't really exist, but I still buy into some of her strategies and slogans. Only, in my reality, nothing seems to work out the way I have planned. I get out crafts to do with the kids and Abby eats everything she can reach: crayons, paint, chalk, stamps…you name it, she'll eat it. On a rainy day, I set up a tent in the living room for the kids to play in. They take turns trying to knock it down until I get fed up and take it down again. Nothing is as easy and fun as it seems like it should be. Supermom has got some great ideas, but my reality is not measuring up. And I'm tired of trying.

May Journal Entry | Abby: 10 ½ months old

I have just come out of an emotional slump that lasted over a week and had me questioning my career path (you know, the one where I gave up my teaching job to become a stay-at-home mother): *I'm not having fun anymore. This year has been so hard and now I have the baby blues when Abby's hardly even a baby anymore. I love my kids so much and I want so badly to be a good mom. But how can I believe I'm a good mom when being around my kids seems to make me depressed sometimes? What am I doing wrong? Maybe I should put the kids in daycare and go back to teaching. Maybe I'm not cut out to be a stay-at-home mom!*

Naturally, I share my angst with Adel. As my loving husband, he is the sole bearer of every single emotional whim I happen upon. He's quite used to it, having been privy to my mood swings for nearly ten years now. Being part robot himself (he's a true engineer), it is difficult for him to feel any real empathy for my emotions, but he listens when I complain and that's usually good enough. The problem is, he tends to have a low tolerance for my self pity (I can't imagine why). So he endures my complaints about this year for the hundredth time:

Me: I just can't understand why I'm not feeling happy.

Adel: Uh huh.

Me: I keep asking myself if I would be happier if I went back to work.

Adel: Uh huh.

227

Me: But then I think about how hard it would be to go to work all day long and then pick up the kids from daycare, somehow survive dinner, cram in some quality time before bedtime, and then do it all again the next day.

Adel: Uh huh.

Me: And teaching was so stressful. I can't imagine adding the stresses of teaching to the stresses of motherhood. I think I'd have a breakdown.

Adel: You're already having a breakdown.

Me: (rolling my eyes) I mean a real breakdown. I just don't think I can handle being a working mom right now. But I'm not sure I'm handling being a stay-at-home mom so well either!

Adel: Uh huh. Keep talking. I'm just going to lean back and close my eyes for a little bit.

Me: Knock it off! I'm trying to figure out if I need to change anything in my life so that I can feel happy.

Silence.

He didn't ask the question to be rude. He simply pointed out the obvious truth that life is not always about being *happy*. So maybe he's not the most compassionate listener, but at least he's sometimes a little bit right. Sometimes the tasks you are assigned are fun and sometimes you just have to suck it up and do them. In reality, I'm quite exceptional at finding pockets of discontent no matter what my situation happens to be. So I'm not sure making a career change would actually help. Perhaps I'm in a season of child-rearing when I just have to hold out to get to the rainbow on the other side.

Later, we went on a family stroll around the block. Isaac, in his *Thomas the Train* helmet, was riding his tricycle up ahead with Adel's help. I held Bitsy's leash while pushing Abby in the umbrella stroller. We stopped to look at the two brown Boxers who silently peered at us over a low-rising fence. We pointed out the colored chalk drawings on the sidewalk. We made sure for the hundredth time that Isaac avoided the giant anthills. We talked with Isaac about robots, moon landers, and Zurg. He stopped to tell us about the cracks in the sidewalk. Abby held my cell phone up to her ear to say "hi." She grinned every time Daddy looked back and smiled at her.

Suddenly, the gray cloud over my head cleared. I realized, *this is it! This is the moment I don't want to miss. These simple repetitive pleasures are what it's all about. There is nothing I want to do that's more important than being with my children. There's nothing in life I want to be right now other than a wife and a mom! So it's hard sometimes! So what? Would I trade anything to miss this moment? No way!*

June Journal Entry | Abby: Almost 12 months old

Abby is weaned!!! Today I went to the doctor to get a prescription for birth control pills and acne medicine (hooray on both counts!) I also mentioned to the doctor my concerns over these periodic bouts of depression:

Megan: I understood feeling that way when I first had Abby, but she's nearly a year old now. Shouldn't "the blues" be long gone?

Doctor: Not necessarily. Let me ask you some questions first. Does your depression have a pattern, such as a regularly occurring time of day?

Megan: Yes! It usually hits at about four in the afternoon, right when the kids wake up from their naps. In the afternoon, I often feel frustrated that I didn't get more done during my "me" time. Sometimes the feeling goes away quickly and sometimes it lingers and becomes depression that I can't seem to shake. And miraculously, it always goes away as soon as the kids are snug in their beds!

Doctor: Imagine yourself doing something else other than sitting at home with your kids during those times when you feel blue. If you were doing that activity instead of taking care of your kids, would that make the feeling of depression go away?

Megan: (*imagining sipping a pina colada on a white-sanded beach next to my dark and handsome husband and hoping the good doctor is about to offer me a plane ticket*) Yep, I'm pretty sure that would help!

Doctor: Then what you're experiencing sounds more like "circumstantial" or "situational" depression. True depression lingers, regardless of circumstances. Added to that is the fact that you just weaned your baby. Nursing is about as hard on a woman's hormones as pregnancy. It will take some time for your hormones to regulate themselves. But there's a lot you can do in the meantime to overcome minor depression. How often do you exercise?

Megan: (*thinking to myself*) Here we go. (*Out loud*) Well, sometimes days in a row and sometimes not for weeks.

Doctor: It's really important that you take care of yourself. You'd be amazed at how many pills we can avoid having to take simply by taking better care of ourselves. Also, be thinking of something different you could do during that vulnerable hour. Listen to music.

Plan an outing or activity. Shake up your routine in order to shake off that gloomy feeling.

I nod my head in agreement. It's so annoying when you know someone is right and you knew it even before they said it, but have been too lame to act on your own knowledge until they nudge you into action. Having the doctor validate my feelings also helps me a great deal. My feelings of depression have made me doubt that I am a good mom. It is comforting to know that what I have been experiencing is a real, physical issue, not just evidence of my failures.

Armed with my newfound knowledge of circumstantial depression, I vow to make a new start. I have realized that if I don't actively engage "the blues" in battle, they have already won! So, I plan to find a way to exercise three to five days a week, rain or shine. I plan to creatively find a way to make my afternoons work for me. And I will make it a priority for every day to include time for me to spend in God's healing presence. With God's help, and a little borrowed wisdom, I am positive I can shake the blues for good and make the days more enjoyable for all of us.

A PROMISE

"Now may the God of hope fill you with all joy and peace in believing, that you may abound in hope by the power of the Holy Spirit" (Romans 15:13).

A PRAYER

Lord, this has felt like a long, slow struggle through murky waters to get to the clarity and hope I have reached today. I have spent so much time lately feeling sorry for myself, time that I could have been using to bring joy to myself and my family. Please help me to take better care of myself so that I can be a better person for my family. And please fill me with Your hope and joy and peace as I face each new day.

Note:

The addition of regular exercise, daily quiet times reading the Bible and praying, and some new ideas for shaking up the afternoon made a clear impact on the number of days per month that I felt gloomy. However, it took another few months after weaning Abby before the gloom went away entirely. I was surprised how long it lasted after weaning and was so relieved when I one day was able to look back on many weeks and realize it was finally gone. I guess it can sometimes take the hormones quite a bit of time to get back to normal. And I'm sure it helped that the kids were getting older and easier to handle too!

First Birthday

I recently finished reading *The Poisonwood Bible* by Barbara Kingsolver. It is a fictional account of a missionary family whose mother struggles under the burden of isolated and unsupported motherhood. She became pregnant with twins very shortly after the birth of her first child. As you can imagine, she was overwhelmed and overrun by the constant demands of her three young ones. Here's Kingsolver's description (unbelievably, it's even more dramatic than my own descriptions of desperate motherhood):

> The twins came just as Rachel was learning to walk. What came next I hardly remember, whole years when I battled through every single day of grasping hands and mouths until I could fall into bed for a few short hours and dream of being eaten alive in small pieces. I counted to one hundred as I rocked, contriving the patience to get one down in order to take up another. One mouth closed on a spoon meant two crying empty, feathers flying, so I dashed back and forth like a mother bird, flouting nature's maw with a brood too large. I

couldn't count on survival until all three of them could stand alone. (381)

If that doesn't make you stressed out just reading it, nothing will! To compare this mother's struggle with my own is like comparing a marathon to a morning jog. It makes me see how easy I've got it. I only have two kids, while this desperate mother had three. My husband is supportive and loving and thoughtful, while hers was demeaning and chauvinistic. I am accustomed to disposable diapers, washing machines, clothes dryers, dishwashers, and lightweight vacuum cleaners, while she was raising her babies with the limited "modern" conveniences of the 1950's. And I now have a wonderful community of support, while this woman was left to forge through each day relentlessly alone. Really, we're nothing alike. But, in my most challenging moments as a mother of two, I can at least relate to the feelings of inescapable, constant effort which she describes so well (and sometimes being eaten alive in small pieces would feel like a welcome respite from my chaos).

In the beginning of this journey, when Isaac was fighting sleep and Abby was so new and helpless, I often felt overwhelmed and overrun. Then, as Isaac slowly settled back into a sleep routine and Abby slowly grew into a little more independence, I went from feeling *overwhelmed* to simply *consumed*. I became adept at caring for my two children, but it took so much effort that I could not accomplish anything else. That bothered me a lot more than it probably should have and I grappled with my lack of contentment and patience.

This past year has felt like an uphill endeavor and, in my mind, Abby's first birthday marks the apex. Now I can begin the downhill slide, slowly picking up momentum day after day, toward peace in my heart and home. I have tried to make the best of each day of this journey. And there were many, *many* moments of beautiful warmth and joy. But I found myself in the more challenging moments chanting this mantra (adjusting the amount of time, of course, based on how old Abby was at the time of my chanting): "In a month and a half, Abby turns one. A month and a half. A month and a half. A month and a half...If only I can survive until we get there!"

And here we are! Abby has just turned one, eaten her cupcake, and is officially a toddler now! I've been to this landmark before and I know what this next year brings. It brings walking and talking. It brings *playing* with toys instead of just trying to *eat* them. Abby is now at the age where she is beginning to "stand alone" and I can feel the grip of her dependence loosening from me. By the end of this next year, Abby will no longer be a baby; she will become a little girl. Her dough-ball rolls will slowly unfold and her curled up posture will lengthen and straighten into the stance of active childhood. Not only that, but I will no longer have a baby and a kid. I will have *kids*! Their sleeping, eating, playing, and bathing needs will be pretty much the same. It's simplicity! It's bliss!

And that is why, when my friend Kristie asked me if I am sad about Abby turning one, I nearly choked on my cupcake. I wanted to shout with glee, "Are you kidding? I've been waiting for this moment all year!" However, prompted by Kristie's sincere expression, I toned down my response. I told her the truth: that I mostly feel relief to have made it this far and I'm sure the sadness will come much later when it's all behind me. Someday I'll miss my kids being in the prime of their snuggly infancies. But right now I am just beginning to feel liberation from my year-long effort to arise from every challenging moment with a little bit of grace.

Looking into Kristie's earnest eyes, I can see that we are mothers who have been undertaking two very different journeys. Kristie appears to have truly taken joy in every moment with her daughter. I am a little envious of that. It seems like that is how motherhood *should* be. For me, motherhood this past year has required a tremendous effort and joy has not always been the first emotion to spring to my mind! (Although it *should* have been!) It amazes me how many times this year I have had to be reminded of the *same things*: take joy in your children, Megan; lean on the Lord for strength, Megan; it's okay to be overwhelmed, Megan...God loves you anyway.

In fact, God probably *wants* you to be overwhelmed, Megan, because it's the only way you will stop and listen to that fact...*God loves you anyway.* You may be exhausted from keeping up with your children, but persevere in this: *God loves you anyway.* You may be lacking in patience and contentment, but strengthen your character in this: *God loves you anyway.* You may have made many mistakes as a mother, but hope in this: *God loves you anyway.* It may be disheartening that you sometimes find motherhood to be a challenge rather than the joyful privilege that it is, but glory in this: *God loves you anyway!*

A PROMISE

"And not only that, but we also glory in tribulations, knowing that tribulation produces perseverance; and perseverance, character; and character, hope" (Romans 5:3-4).

A PRAYER

Lord, I am so thankful to You for helping me make it to this point in one piece! I will always cherish the growth that was prompted by the challenges of this year. Even more so, I am grateful beyond description for the truly joyful privilege it is to raise my beautiful children in Your name. Help me to cherish every moment I have with them while they are still young and to expand my horizons wisely as they continue to grow in independence. I ask You to continue to use my weakness to help me learn perseverance, to strengthen my character, and to cause me to hope in You alone!

Happy Anniversary

I haven't been writing too much about Adel these days. Maybe a passage here or there on how he reacts to my daily challenges, but that's about it. It's very indicative of where the majority of my attention and energy is focused right now. I spend my days feeding, corralling, consoling, compromising with, playing with, and caring for my kids. When Adel gets home, we strain to get our words in edgewise as we greet each other and try to listen for the answer to the question, "How was your day?" As simple as that question is, we're not always successful in completing a response.

It is a nightly challenge to hold a conversation with my husband. Generally it's dinnertime when he comes home. We step over toys and dodge children who are trying to climb up our legs as we microwave, bake, boil, or sauté our way through the quickest possible meal preparations. Abby can typically be found blaring her repetitious monologue: "Dada! Dada! Dada!" Or, if she's really hungry: "More-more! More-more! More thaaaat!" And Isaac is usually vocalizing about whatever happens to cross his whimsical, hypersensitive mind. It is a daily struggle to make Adel a priority with all the voices that bellow for attention in this house.

And let's not even begin to talk about intimacy! What's that?! By bedtime, I'm ready to crawl in bed and succumb to a coma-like state. Intimacy is about as far from my mind as professional football. But Adel is a man. And, as every wife knows, men have "reserve energy tanks" just for restful moments such as these. Quite frankly, I'm exhausted and have done a terrible job of preserving any shred of energy for my husband. That is why, this year more than ever, I want to plan a day or two away from it all for the both of us.

This month marks our six-year anniversary. My parents agreed to keep both kids for a day or two so Adel and I could enjoy each other's company. We decided to take advantage of our empty house and just stay home and be together. As I planned our weekend, I looked forward with relish to the day when I would drive the kids up to my mom's house and leave them there. I was so excited at the thought of someone else taking diligent care of my children's ever-incessant needs so that Adel and I could remind each other that we're actually mildly interesting people.

When the day finally arrived, however, I found myself stalling at the door of Mimi's house. I realized, without too much surprise, that I was going to miss my kids. I also realized, again, that my mom is a saint and was going to have more than her hands full for the next day or two. I realized that Abby and Isaac would do fine without me for a while, although I knew Isaac would have his "I want my mommy!" meltdowns. Finally, I realized that I had better walk out that door before Mimi changed her mind and made me take both kids back home with me!

The drive home was…quiet. I'm not used to silence in the car and it was strange and pleasant. I thought uninterrupted thoughts and sang old, familiar songs to amuse myself. When I got home, I spent twenty minutes picking up the remaining clutter from our home. I wanted this weekend to be stress-free, and for me that me that means everything in its place. Having completed my quick clean-up, I looked around and found all the things I had put away in *exactly the place where I had put them*! Now that's different! I'm so used to things unraveling themselves right behind me that I was strangely gratified at the effectiveness of my small efforts.

After this last bit of "work" I enjoyed a steaming hot bath to wash away the worries and grime of the commute and the week. Then, I *primped*. This novelty was so enjoyable that I kept adding long-ignored steps to my regimen. I spent half an hour just curling my hair. Then I plucked my eyebrows, did my make up, and spent another thirty minutes trying on every dress in my closet to see which ones still fit. I finally selected a jean skirt and cute v-neck top. I moisturized and then accessorized. And I even rummaged through the bins below the sink to find the perfume Adel gave me a few years ago. By the end I felt casual and comfortable, but flirty and romantic too. Sometimes being a mom is so consuming that it's easy to forget that I'm also a *woman*. But after *only* two hours of primping, I was ready to claim that feminine title again.

Soon it was time for dinner. Although we'd been talking sushi for about a week in advance, I finally decided that margaritas are (in some cases) far more important than actual food, so we settled on the local Mexican restaurant. Over dinner, we talked. We talked about his work, about our fun new friends, about the kids, about our family, about my writing, about our plans for the future. We joked about our idiosyncrasies, the ones that attract us to each other and drive us crazy at the same time. We laughed and remembered together, and we felt like friends again.

We also reminisced about our wedding:

Megan: This time six years ago we were eating a king-sized snickers bar in the bathtub of the hotel room after our wedding reception.

Adel: This time six years ago we were getting ready for our Alaskan cruise honeymoon.

Megan: This time six years ago I was skinny!

Adel: You're still beautiful.

And after months and days of slowly losing each other to the intensity of parenting, we found each other again in a few quiet moments.

The next day, as we got in the car to pick up the kids, I began to comprehend many things that I hadn't really thought about before. For one, I work very hard every day, so much so that it's easy to lose the woman that I am inside the mother I have become. What's more, while I like my "job," I immensely enjoyed the break from the constant serving and sacrificing that is required. These breaks are good, and it is so important to have time to focus on my husband, and myself, without child-interference. I was also acutely aware that I missed my kids and as much as they may drive me crazy and keep me off balance, I was so glad to bring them back home. Finally, I reminded myself how important it is not to let my marriage get lost in the shuffle. My husband is worth the effort.

A PROMISE
"My beloved spoke, and said to me: 'Rise up, my love, my fair one, and come away...O my dove, in the clefts of the rock, in the secret places of the cliff, let me see your face, let me hear your voice; for your voice is sweet, and your face is lovely'" (Song of Solomon 2:10,14).

A PRAYER
Lord, I know that You created marriage to be the cornerstone for the health and well-being of any family, and that You intended a

good, healthy marriage to represent Your love to the world. I confess that for far too long I have been taking it for granted that, without any effort, my marriage would remain vibrant and healthy. Thank You for allowing us the opportunity to reconnect and rekindle our love. Please help me to make changes in my routine that will allow my husband to become more of a daily priority.

Miracle

A PERSPECTIVE

Having read of my earlier attempts to do such commonplace activities as buying necessities at Target or taking the dog to the vet, you may understand that I have built up a natural aversion to any such outing with my children. In fact, for the past year, I have mostly been avoiding combining a store of any kind with my two kids unless it was absolutely necessary for our survival.

However, today I wanted to buy some paint and some wooden letters for Abby's door. Isaac's door is decorated with his name in nicely painted letters and I just know it won't be much longer before Abby says, "Hey, where are *my* letters?" I'm still trying to battle the old "second child syndrome" thing. It will be an endless fight, I know. But, in an attempt to restore some balance to the precariously-uneven tilt of sibling equality in our household, I took the kids to the craft store this morning. What followed was a delightful series of events that, to me, were nothing short of a miracle (thus the title).

My miracle today was that, upon attempting this trip to the craft store with my kids, *we all had a pleasant time*. Seriously! That's it! But I can't tell you enough how much hope it gave me. Perhaps this is evidence that I am indeed on my way up out of the bog?

Perhaps our little family unit is working its way toward functioning in a normal, public setting?

Here's how it went:

Isaac walked beside the cart, marveling at the brightly colored craft supplies. Before we entered, I told him he didn't have to sit in the cart as long as he didn't pull things off the shelves. He was wonderfully behaved. No tantrums. No disasters. No drawing on Mommy's rear end with lipstick. Just his constant, fascinated babblings about the fun crafts on each shelf: "Oooo...Look at this Mom!" When it came time to pick out the paints, he helped me locate the colors that I needed.

Abby, too, was well behaved. She sat in the cart, looking around. A few times she told me she was "mina" (finished) but she never fussed or complained. On the whole, we had fun exploring and making our selections. And we were in and out within half an hour's time.

Amazingly, things are really starting to run smoothly around here. Abby is now fourteen months old, running away when I try to catch her for a diaper change and running to me when I announce it's time for "more-more" (time to eat!).

Isaac will turn three in just two weeks. He's way into super heroes right now, thanks to the plethora of library books we've been toting home with characters like Spiderman, Batman, and the Transformers. And he's actually starting to behave more like a big boy these days. Occasionally, I get glimpses of what kind of a person he's growing into:

Mommy: Where are you, Isaac?

Isaac: I'm upstairs. (*Oh my gosh, is he playing independently?!*)

Mommy: Do you see Abby?

Isaac: She's right here. (*Oh my gosh, is he keeping track of his little sister?!*)

He's starting to take responsibility, not only for himself, but also for his little sister. One day recently, he put away, without my asking, all the baskets that Abby pulled off the shelf. I'm drifting into mommy heaven! And the first time he said "Okay Mom" instead of throwing a tantrum, I nearly fainted. I once again find myself asking, "Who is this child?" Only this time I'm liking the changes I see!

We have settled into a lovely routine. Every day is pretty much the same. It's predictable. It's safe and easy. It gives me such a lovely feeling of peace when things go smoothly and everyone is getting along! It feels as if, after struggling uphill through crazy terrain, I suddenly look up to find myself in a clearing. Ah, I have a moment to catch my breath!

As I described this feeling to my Aunt Teri, she was quick to point out that it was not simply the passage of time that was making things go so much more smoothly. While acknowledging that the children's ages do make a difference, she also congratulated...*me*...on a job well done: "I feel that you are reaping the fruit of godly investments in your precious children......investments in the form of loving discipline, hard work, and patience. Good job, Mom and Dad!!"

Honestly, before she said that, it had never occurred to me that our more-peaceful existence of late had anything to do with (gasp!) *me*. Though I hesitate to admit it, there's a part of me that feels a little swelling of pride in hearing those words of encouragement. It is breathtaking to think that Adel and I, while huffing and struggling through the rocky terrain, have looked to God for guidance, called out daily to Him for help, and are now beginning to reap the reward of our efforts and our trust in Him! As the months go by, my rough days really are spreading farther and farther apart. I can feel our family emerging, by God's good grace, from our uphill battle to a journey of relative peace! It truly is getting better!

A PROMISE

"And let us not grow weary while doing good, for in due season we shall reap if we do not lose heart" (Galatians 6:9).

A PRAYER

Lord, I cannot tell You how grateful I am that I can see a definitive improvement in our daily family life. I feel like peace is being restored to our home and I know You are here with us, helping us as we all learn and grow together. We do not want to get weary now, but stay strong in our parenting efforts, so that we can reap the greater reward when our kids, by Your grace, grow into godly people shaped by our hard work.

Gender Neutral?

A PERSPECTIVE

As the four of us were driving home from church recently, Isaac explained matter-of-factly, "Boys don't play with ponies." Suppressing a giggle at his sudden observation, I asked him where he heard that. He told me one of his Sunday school teachers had told him. Then, instead of a giggle, I found myself suppressing a hint of indignation that someone would say that to a near three-year-old boy. Do we really need to precondition such young boys and girls to what is gender appropriate? Sure that the teacher had been teasing him, I shook it off and explained that he could play with ponies if he wanted to. But it started me thinking. How do I define what is gender appropriate for my children? And what exactly is the difference between boys and girls anyway?

Nearly a year ago, I took my kids to a nearby indoor play area. Two-year-old Isaac was running around enjoying the freedom and new toys. Abby was slumped in my lap, attempting to look like something other than a bobble-head doll. She was just a few months old and had that short, standup-ish, newborn hair that makes it hard to tell if the baby is a boy or a girl (my friend Jen calls this type of newborn hair "chicken fuzz").

While I sat holding Abby, a curious pre-school-aged girl approached us. She was interested in the baby. After a few preliminary questions, the girl asked if the baby was a boy or a girl.

"She's a girl," I said. "Her name is Abby."

True to the why-minded curiosity of her age group, the girl then asked, "Why is she a girl?"

Well, that's a silly question, I thought. *How am I supposed to answer that without getting technical, and maybe in trouble with her mother?* Other than the fact that Isaac loved to roughhouse and could make really cool sound effects involving lots of projectile spit, I wasn't sure I knew how to describe the difference between boys and girls.

So I turned the question back on the child: "Why are *you* a girl?"

The girl stared at me blankly, as if not comprehending the question she herself had just asked. I rephrased, "What do you have that makes you a girl?" I swear I was not looking for the scientific explanation. I was thinking along the lines of long hair, dresses, sugar and spice and everything nice.

After a moment's pause to think, the girl responded, "What do I have that makes me a girl? Perfume!" So *that's* what little girls are made of!

As a one-year-old girl, Abby is proving herself to be delicate, gentle, and ultra-feminine, gracefully holding her arm in the air as she prances around the house wearing a shiny bracelet. And she could not stop looking at her feet the day she got her first pretty pink pedicure from Aunt Robin.

However, she has also demonstrated her ability to keep up with her older brother. She's no pushover and certainly no pansy. Among Abby's first phrases was "bad guys!" And she makes a tremendous "roar" sound effect for dinosaurs or anything that remotely

247

resembles any living creature. What fourteen-month-old girl can claim those unusual skills? Only one who has an older brother! She will fearlessly engage in tug-o-war battles with Isaac over a toy, both of them shouting, "Mine!" And when roughhousing with Isaac, she usually doesn't seem to mind getting bowled over. What can I say? She's a tough cookie.

In fact, if anyone ends up crying it's usually Isaac: "Abby took my toy!" or "Abby pushed me!" Admittedly, my daughter is going through a bit of a bully stage. It's going to take some training to teach her to be loving and gentle and kind while still maintaining her healthy sense of self.

And, in all honesty, my son is going through a bit of a cry-baby stage. Now that he and Abby are on a level playing field, he seems to view acting the "victim" as a great way to get mommy's attention. But it worries me a little. If he can't defend himself from his baby sister, how is he going to survive preschool? And don't even think about middle school! It's going to take more than a little training to teach him to stand up for himself and become a leader while maintaining his healthy gentleness and sensitivity.

When it comes down to it, I want my children to be given equal opportunities, regardless of their gender. If he wants to play with My Little Ponies instead of army men, that's fine. But I also want my son to know that God has a special plan in mind for him because he is a little boy. He will one day grow into a man. And I want him to be *such* a man! I want him to know what it means to be a man of conviction, a *godly* man.

A man like his Boppa. No one would ever accuse my father of being anything other than a man. He stands for principles higher than himself and he does not back down in the face of opposition. His faith in God, leading by example, along with his and my mother's commitment to always be involved in our youth group experiences, largely influenced both my sister's and my close walks of faith that we enjoy today. In high school, he stopped a bully from beating up a smaller kid, promising to meet the big guy later to finish it off. When they met up again, my dad refused to fight, although he was pushed around by the bully before the guy lost interest and left him alone. And yet, this same man is willing to be dressed up as a fairy queen by his grandchildren, earrings, necklaces, tiara, wings, and magic wand included. Now *that* is a man!

If my daughter decides to play sword fight rather than baby dolls, that's okay too. After all, her momma was a tomboy until age fifteen, only then realizing that it took way too much effort to be tough and officially becoming a wimp. So if my little girl is a tough cookie, that's okay with me. But I also want her to know that God has a special plan in mind for her because she is a little girl. She will one day grow into a woman. And I want her to be *such* a woman! I want her to know what it means to be a woman of character, a *godly* woman.

A woman like Queen Esther. There are only two books in the entire Bible that are primarily about women, so women would do well to learn from them (and teach them to their daughters)! Esther was a beautiful young Jewish woman who was selected to be queen. Sounds pretty fluffy and feminine, right? However, her uncle asked her to use her influence with the king, despite the risk, to keep her people from being destroyed: "For if you remain completely silent at this time, relief and deliverance will arise for the Jews from another place, but you and your father's house will perish. Yet who knows whether you have come to the kingdom for such a time as this?"(Esther 4:14). So, feminine Esther mans up and risks her life for her people: "And so I will go to the king, which is against the law; and if I perish, I perish" (Esther 4:15b). And yet she does it in the most womanly way possible: she invites the king to a feast! The woman uses her feminine hospitality. The king falls for it. The good guys win. The bad guys bite the dust. All because Esther was a woman of character, a godly woman. Or, as one joke says, a woman who, when she gets up in the morning, causes Satan to say, "Oh crap! She's up!"

A PROMISE

"So God created man in His own image; in the image of God He created him; male and female He created them" (Genesis 1:27).

A PRAYER

Lord, though we strive for equality between the sexes, there is something special about a little boy or a little girl. There is a reason You created both male *and* female in Your image. Help us to shape our son into a man who will bring You honor and glory. Help us to shape our daughter into a woman who will bring You pride and joy.

Birthday Parties

A PERSPECTIVE

Isaac is turning three in a few days! He has been to a fair share of birthday parties this past year and knows what it means to be the "birthday boy." I think he would really enjoy a party just for him this year.

The thing that gives me this impression is that at every birthday party we've been to lately, Isaac has managed to wiggle himself right up to the birthday boy or girl's side. He will pick up the unopened presents, wondering excitedly, "What's inside?" He becomes the "errand boy" or "present elf," delivering the presents one by one to the birthday kid, much faster than the kid can actually open them. If it's a gift bag, Isaac will stuff his head inside the bag as the kid tries to pull out whatever is inside.

Consequently, most of the photographs taken by the birthday kid's parents end up looking something like this:

- Two pictures of the back of Isaac's head as he hands a present to the birthday boy.
- Three pictures of half of the birthday boy's face as he watches from behind while Isaac stuffs his whole head into another gift bag.

- Five pictures of Isaac looking at the camera, holding up the next present. The birthday boy's elbow or ear is generally visible in the background.
- Nine pictures of Isaac's mother pulling Isaac away from the pile of presents.
- Twenty actual pictures of the birthday boy opening a present. Unfortunately, these pictures are all of the kid opening the *same* present, shot in rapid-fire succession, because it was the last present and Isaac was finally dragged outside by his aggravated mother.

So, it's fairly safe to say that Isaac is looking forward to his own birthday party this year. On the other hand, so am I. I have been daydreaming of fun birthday themes and ideas. (I secretly believe that one of the best things about having kids is that it gives me the excuse to *play* again. Whenever we, I mean, *my children*, get a new toy, I have to "conquer" the toy immediately. It is essential that I push every button and pull every lever to discover the ins and outs of each new toy. Then my kids can have a turn.) So admittedly, Isaac's birthday party this year will be as much for the childish mother as it is for the child himself.

When planning a party, I have learned that there are two extremes I can take. The first approach would be to order the biggest and baddest of everything to insure that everyone knows that *I* know how to throw a party. I could order a giant bounce house, pony rides, "characters" to walk around scaring the children, face painters, food vendors, tattoo artists, presidential candidates for schmoozing, etc. Of course, then I would be sacrificing Isaac's future for the sake of one afternoon's entertainment. I can imagine my eighteen-year-old son, spoiled rotten by years of over-zealous birthday parties, stomping his size fourteen shoe and whining nasally, "Mom, why didn't you order the clowns and presidential candidates for my first birthday party at college?" (Isn't that cute?) To which I would have to reply, "Son, after years of paying for extravagant birthday parties, we can no longer afford for you to go to college, period. So pack up your things and join the army."

Instead of this drastic outcome, I could opt for the second extreme of child parties: ghetto-cheap everything. This means that I would make everything myself: the cake, the decorations, the favors, the invitations, and the food. The idea here is to skip all the hoopla and get back to the basics of birthday fun. The downside to this is that everyone would know *for sure* that I am the cheapest human being alive and will think twice before returning to another one of my parties.

Then there's the guests. Ah, guests. This is the next great puzzle to solve when planning a child's birthday party. Who should be included on the guest list? There are so many options and so many ways to offend people that it makes the task of setting a guest list quite daunting. I have had numerous conversations with my friends on this subject. Through these conversations I have found we are all strong of opinion and there is indeed no "right" answer to the question of what is appropriate for the birthday party of a young child.

For example, as far as guest lists are concerned, there are two options: 1. invite everyone you know and 2. limit your guest list. To further study the pros and cons of these two options, I am including the following table:

	Option 1: Invite Everyone You Know	Option 2: Limit Your Guest List
Pros	✓ No one will be left out or get their feelings hurt ✓ More new toys for you, I mean, for *your kid* to play with	✓ Smaller, more intimate group ✓ Less hoopla and chaos ✓ Less excess ✓ Cuts costs

	Option 1: Invite Everyone You Know	Option 2: Limit Your Guest List
Cons	✓ Too many presents (Is that possible?) ✓ Reduces college savings ✓ Reinforces child's inborn assumption that he is the center of the universe	✓ Increased chance of having your child receive a curse from a wicked fairy

In Option 1, you invite everyone you know in order to avoid hurting feelings and leaving someone out. By inviting everyone, I mean *everyone*: your work friends, your church friends, your playgroup friends, your neighborhood friends, your workout friends, your dog park friends, and your mafia friends. This would insure that you would not leave anyone out. Plus you would have a really good reason for buying a bigger house, such as Hearst Castle.

The second option is to trim down the guest list in an effort to avoid hoopla and extravagance. Inevitably this will result in hurt feelings. Just be sure not to exclude any bad fairies because, as we all learned from Maleficent's example, bad fairies are really poor sports. In my case, I think as long as I'm careful, I'll opt for keeping my child's birthday party list limited to the closest friends of the *child* (crazy idea, I know!). Isaac is probably not interested in socializing with my mafia friends anyway. But, after his birthday has passed, if I'm still aching to have a party that includes my mafia friends, then I can simply host a party *for* my mafia friends.

So, after *way* too much thought (as usual), my plan is to ere on the side of ghetto-cheapness and risk being cursed by the bad fairies. Isaac is going to have a pirate-themed party this year. I plan to cut up our old moving boxes and paint the cardboard into a pirate ship that the kids can play in. This should turn out *great* since I pretty much have the artistic ability of a turnip. I'll invite a few families from the neighborhood whose kids Isaac has gotten to know pretty well.

Even with these limitations, I still tend to get carried away with inspiration and elaborate creativity. As I get caught up in the excitement of planning, I think the most important thing for me to remember is the reason for the occasion. Although I love getting creative with a good idea, I don't want to get so lost in the details that I forget the fact that we're celebrating a huge milestone in my child's life. We will be celebrating the joyous fact that Isaac has now officially grown out of the terrible twos! Wahoo!

A PROMISE

"So this day shall be to you a memorial; and you shall keep it as a feast to the Lord throughout your generations. You shall keep it as a feast by an everlasting ordinance" (Exodus 12:14).

A PRAYER

Lord, I spend *way* too much time thinking about and planning things. It can be so much fun to daydream about events like birthday parties. However, I want to remember that the day is special, not because of how much of a fuss I make over it, but because it is a memorial. We remember and celebrate the day that the perfect Gift-Giver blessed us with the most miraculous gift. Thank You for this child!

255

Evolution of a Father

When Adel and I first started our parenting journey, I never imagined how different we both would be three years later. In the pages of this book alone, there is example after example of how I have struggled and matured in my mothering. With much less pageantry, Adel has been silently engaging in his own growth as a father.

Adel has been an involved, loving father from day one. He has never shied away from changing diapers, wiping boogies, or night-long rocking fests. And he is exceptionally gifted at playing with our children at every stage of their development.

However, there was one thing that my husband was very hesitant to do for quite some time when Isaac was a baby: *be in charge*! Adel was comfortable accompanying and assisting me in the endless task of mothering the baby. He was willing for me to run out on a quick errand or activity, leaving a well-fed, well-rested Isaac in his care (with an extended list of instructions for daddy's use in case baby should start to cry). But, it was an entirely different ball-game when I would ask Adel to actually be in charge of the baby for a while.

Being in charge means that *he* would have to figure out when and how to feed, clothe, change, sleep, and entertain the baby. It might

256

mean that daddy would have to take the child on an outing, just the two of them. In the first two years of Isaac's life, this kind of fatherly behavior was unheard of in our household! Sure, I suggested it a few times, but the idea of being in charge was just a little bit daunting for this new father. And I, being the new mother, did not want to push Adel (or the baby!) too hard.

After I had Abby, I realized I needed more help than I was getting. I decided it was time for Daddy to test out his parenting wings. So, when Adel offered to run to the grocery store, I asked him to take twenty-one-month-old Isaac with him. At first Adel wavered. But after a few minutes of listening to my teary assertions (about how overwhelmed I was with a newborn and a toddler, and how I needed more help now that we had two kids, *and* how it was helpful that he went to the store, but what I really needed was someone to entertain Isaac) he decided that surely it would be easier to manage the child than the momma!

Thus, Adel stepped into the challenging world of *being in charge* of our first-born child. Just as I had done from the beginning of my parenting experience, Adel made mistakes. And just as I had done from the beginning, Adel learned from his mistakes and grew in comfort and confidence. Before long, he had mastered being in charge of one child.

But of course, we have *two* children. Therein lies the next problem. Adel had to rapidly learn to be in charge of *both* our children. I waited a reasonable amount of time before I attempted a mommy's night out event. And since I was nursing Abby, in the early months I would put her down to sleep so that Adel only had to deal with Isaac's bedtime and rock Abby if she woke up.

This worked fine for some time. But life kept on evolving and eventually I needed to leave Adel with both kids *when they were awake*. We were nervous the first time I did this. And rightfully so. Our kids have tag-team parent torture down pat! Still, Adel heroically stepped up time after time to tackle this troublesome duo so mommy could serve at church or attend a baby shower.

Initially when I started leaving Adel in charge of both the kids, I would come home to a madhouse. As soon as I opened the door, the kids would be crying, holding their arms out to me. The house would be a disaster, toys and food strewn everywhere. It would take me quite some time to get everything back in order again. By the time I finished straightening things up, my little outing hardly seemed worth the trauma.

But we pressed on and, eventually, I opened the door to...peace. Adel and the kids would be playing pleasantly upstairs. Discarded toys would be put away and dishes would be rinsed. And then, one day, upon coming home from some mommy-only event, I realized that Adel had really mastered the "father-of-two" thing. That day, when I opened the door, I was greeted by two smiling children and a clean kitchen, smelling beautifully of my favorite cookies that Daddy had helped the kids bake for me while I was gone. It doesn't get much better than this, ladies!

That's not to say that things always go according to "mommy standard" when Daddy's in charge. If Adel has to dress the kids, I'll come home to unmatched, sometimes skuzzy looking children. Recently, I came home to a beaming Abby. She couldn't have been happier, even though she looked like a ragamuffin. It had been a long day of Daddy being in charge, and Abby had at least two meals worth of food mess plastered on her cheeks and chin. Her limbs were self-decorated with six different colors of marker. And her long bangs, left bereft of barrette all day, had fallen over her eyes and become incrusted in the goo that had dried under her nose. And they had been having so much fun that neither Daddy nor daughter had noticed what a state she was in!

It is such a joy to witness my husband maturing as a father. I am so proud of him. But what makes me most proud of this everyday hero is that, when I told him I needed help making my afternoons less dreary, he stepped up to help me. He could have printed out a list a mile long of all the things he already does for me. He could have pointed out the fact that *he* doesn't get any time to himself when he comes home from work. He could have brushed off my feelings with the thoughtless, "you chose this job" comment. Instead, he reacted in sacrificial love for me.

Now, when he comes home from work, he takes the kids outside or upstairs and plays with them for half an hour so I can blessedly cook our dinner in peace. It's such a simple and obvious solution, and I wish we had thought of it sooner. It turns my least favorite chore of the day into a pleasant task. My attitude is so much better for the rest of the evening when I get that little slice of time to myself. Have I mentioned that I love my husband? Well, I do!

A PROMISE

"The steps of a good man are ordered by the Lord, and He delights in his way" (Psalm 37:23).

A PRAYER

Lord, I am so thankful for my loving husband. I am thankful that he is a man of God and is continually growing as our children's father, my husband, and Your child. I pray that He will continue to grow in those areas and that You would bless him.

Workout Chronicles

Exercise for me is a love-hate kind of thing. I love it enough to value it, but I hate that it takes so much time! When does a busy mother exercise? One of my rules is that any exercising must be done while my children are awake. I'm not going to waste precious nap time, my few moments of prized freedom, on sweating. It's a good rule, but it can make it tricky to get exercise. This entry is the chronicle of my efforts to exercise and lose my pregnancy weight over the course of Abby's first year (and beyond!).

1. The "Labor and Delivery" Workout:

Don't roll your eyes! Labor *is* a workout. And you lose weight so I'm totally counting it. I gained roughly forty pounds during my second pregnancy. After I had Abby, I held onto an extra fifteen pounds for many months. (And I'm not counting the five pounds I never lost after having Isaac!)

Timeframe	Weight Left to Lose
June 7: Abby is born	15 lbs (meaning, I am left with an extra fifteen pounds after expelling the baby, along with all the other baby-related paraphernalia)

2. The "Sorry Excuse for a Denise Austin" Workout:

A few months after Abby was born, I decided that I had let the "newborn excuse" ride for long enough, and it was time I started exercising again. It was quite out of the question for me to resume my former outdoor walking until the wet and sticky armpit-of-Texas heat abated and the weather became more reasonable. So I decided to try an exercise video.

The attempt was disastrous. For one thing, I was inadequately prepared. The exercise ball I had bought over a year before would no longer hold its shape as a result of being left for months on end in the backyard sunlight. It remained warped into an oval no matter how much air I pumped into it. And since I had no actual weights, I had selected two fourteen-ounce cans of refried beans.

For the first five minutes or so, things were going okay, despite my inadequate supplies. On the screen, Denise Austin bubbled at me about how good I was going to look and what a great job I was doing. I was encouraging two-year-old Isaac to follow along and he was having fun flopping all over the floor in attempts to mimic my stretches. Infant Abby was hoisted up on the some pillows so she could watch our performance.

After the first five minutes, my efforts went completely to pot. Had Ms. Austin actually been in the room with me, I'm sure she would have been staring open-mouthed at my laughable attempt to keep up with her. Isaac became bored with trying to follow along and decided he would rather try to climb all over me as I scrambled to keep up with Denise's lunging and kicking. Then Abby started crying because, let's face it, I'm just not that interesting to watch for long periods of time unless you get some misguided enjoyment out of watching a woman with the grace of a buffalo try to dance the tango. After a few minutes of straining to hear Denise over Abby's wails, I finally gave up and picked up the baby, thinking I could one-arm it for the rest of the time. But between Abby's discomfort in my arms, and Isaac clinging to my leg like a baby koala, I decided to throw in the towel, right at Ms. Austin's cheerful grin.

After that one, feeble attempt at exercise, I decided to put it off until after Christmas. Yes, I realize it was only September when I made that first, lame effort to get exercise, but one can't be expected to start a new exercise routine right before the holidays. So I ate my way through Christmas and beyond.

Timeframe	Weight Left to Lose
September-January	Still 15 lbs (actually, *more* than fifteen since I started gaining weight after comfort-eating for months on end)

3. The "Walking" Workout:

I asked for a double jogging stroller for Christmas, and I got it. And the weather was nice so I really had no excuse not to use it. After watching the needle on the scale slowly creeping in the wrong direction, I finally started walking again. I would try to set aside time for a brisk walk, the two kids tucked snugly into my new stroller. Our route was short: just a mile and a half from my door, around the neighborhood lake, and back again. But at least it was *something* and I stopped gaining weight. I even went on a "no dessert" diet that lasted about a month and lost about five pounds from my efforts.

Timeframe	Weight Left to Lose
January-March	10 lbs (thighs starting to rub together a little less these days)

4. The "Kick-It-Up-A-Notch Jogging" Workout:

Over Easter I told my cousin Kelli, who happens to be very svelte even after two babies, that I was planning on stepping up my exercise plan by lengthening my route and adding jogging to my normal morning walk. She encouraged me with these words: "taking care of your physical body does so much for your attitude about life. Looking hot is just a cool side-effect."

My new jogging route was about three miles long and doubled the amount of time I was getting exercise. It was not easy to start. During those first few weeks, my rear end felt cumbersome enough to merit its own zip code. I obviously *looked* like I was performing some grueling feat, making my public efforts to get in shape quite embarrassing. My friend Mac suggested that I jog in a shirt that says, "I'm on my ninth mile, how about you?" That might have helped me feel better!

Kicking up my workout was going nicely for the most part. The only problem was my inconsistency. As I confessed to my doctor during our "baby blues" conversation, some weeks I would exercise five days in a row and some weeks, not at all. But even without consistency, the kicked-up workout seemed to help. Not that I ever looked "hot," but as Kelli indicated, I felt so much more confident and accomplished on the days when I went jogging.

Timeframe	Weight Left to Lose
March-June	5 lbs (can fit into all my shirts and most of my pants, but still none of my dresses and my wedding ring is *still* too tight)

5. The "It's-Too-Hot-To-Go-Jogging-and-I'm-Too-Cheap-to-Get-a-Gym-Membership,-So-Let's-Get-Creative" Workout:

The jogging worked great until the heat really picked up again at the end of June. So from July through September, I engaged in an "alternative" workout. Every morning after breakfast, I gathered my weights (Mom and Dad gave me an old set...no more cans of refried beans!) and my children into the living room. Then we listened to a CD of children's music together.

Encouraging the kids to sing along, I used the length of each song to implement a single exercise move: one song for sit-ups, one song for pushups, one song for leg lifts, three songs for different weight exercises, and a few for marching and dancing with the kids. Of course, Isaac and Abby spent most of the time sitting on the couch watching me like I was their own live-and-in-person TV show. And any time I was on the floor (sit-ups and leg lifts), they fought over who got so sit on top of me. But overall, it was better than my first attempt at in-house exercising.

After this twenty minute "warm up" I would lug the kids into the jogging stroller with sippy cups full of ice water and a towel for my brow. Then I would brave the Texas summer heat for the twenty minutes it took me to walk/jog around the lake and back. It was not the most professional work-out ever, but I had to exercise (by doctor's orders) so it was better than nothing!

Timeframe	Weight Left to Lose
July-September	5 lbs (with my comfort eating, it's just enough effort to hold my weight even)

6. And Finally, The "Manageable Routine" Workout:

Since the weather has cooled down a little after the intense summer heat, I have started my three-mile walking and jogging route again. I love it and the day doesn't feel complete without it. Not only that, but I've kept it up for long enough that I finally dropped those stubborn five pounds!

When the weather gets warm again next summer, I will probably resume my goofy indoor workout (hopefully without the comfort eating this time!). But as long as I am able, I plan to keep up a great exercise routine. This new fit-and-healthy version me is just too good to lose.

Timeframe	Weight Left to Lose
September-?	0 lbs (not that I look like a bikini model, but the extra layer of padding has been sufficiently reduced!)

A PROMISE

"For bodily exercise profits a little, but godliness is profitable for all things, having promise of the life that now is and of that which is to come" (1 Timothy 4:8).

A PRAYER

Lord, help me to persevere in getting daily exercise and making smart choices about what I eat on a daily basis. It sure feels good to fit into my old jeans again! However, make me even more committed to exercising my faith as well, knowing the profits are eternal for that kind of work out.

It Keeps Getting Better

A PERSPECTIVE

My family is now at a comfortable place. Mother, Father, Sister, Brother—all learning together to follow our Creator God in spite of life's hiccups. Daddy does a great job balancing work and family. Mommy is finally content with the daily routine. Big Brother is growing in knowledge and independence. And Sister is growing in speed, aerodynamics, agility, destructive capacity, and general tenacity (just like big brother did right before she was born).

It's true! Now that Abby's approaching 18 months old, she's beginning to exhibit some of those crazy toddler qualities that caught me so off guard with Isaac. Now that she's walking confidently, she struts around picking toilet paper off the near-empty tube like cotton candy. Now *she's* the one emptying the Tupperware out of the cabinet or trying on every pair of shoes in my closet, leaving them strewn about the house. But instead of panicking or feeling overwhelmed and out of control like in the "old days," I now say, "Bring it! I can handle this!" I feel so seasoned now! I'm confident in my mothering skills and in my ability to handle the sticky situations of toddler-parenting.

For example, Abby's starting to pull the "I-don't-want-to-sleep-when-you-tell-me-to-sleep" thing just like her brother used to do. Isaac's bedtime battles caused me huge, motherly insecurity. Was I doing the right thing? Would he be okay? Would it ever end? But with Abby, I actually pretty much know the answers to those questions. No, I'm probably not doing the right thing. Yes, she will be okay anyway. And yes, it will end; everything does eventually.

I even have the luxury this time around of cherishing the fact that my baby needs me. When Isaac needed me back in his sleep-war days, I didn't have the time to snuggle with him endlessly like he desired. I had another baby to tend to. Now that Isaac is such a big boy, sleeping like a champ, Abby pretty much has me to herself (scales of sibling equality temporarily tilting back in her direction!).

Added to my newfound confidence, is the fact that I'm literally more comfortable in my skin than I was eighteen months ago. I've lost the last few pounds that made me feel so unlike myself. With some Christmas gift cards, I was able to treat my new "skinny" self to some pants that actually fit. On top of that, I have won the chemical warfare against my acne. It's wonderful to look like myself again. I may not be a supermodel, but at least I know that people are seeing *me* now instead of the big talking zit.

And somehow, many of the relationships I struggled to begin in my mommy group have matured into genuine friendships. Attending an endless line of birthday parties, baby showers, mommy's night outs, and other events, I one day realized that I was actually comfortable among this group of women. I no longer felt like a stranger trying unsuccessfully to make a name for myself (at least one other than "Frazzle Head"). We are now past the "nice to meet you" stage and into the more personal "growing together" stage of friendship. Sure, none of us are perfect. But that's actually what's so great about a group of dedicated friends. We prop up one another's inadequacies and celebrate one another's strengths.

It is an amazing community of support. We have comforted and cried over loss, carbo-boosted and cheered a marathon run, coddled and cooed many newborns (and many more to come!), provided meals and wisdom for moms newly home from delivering their own second babies, prayed and encouraged through more than one family illness, toasted and cheered over our everyday victories, supported and buoyed through one challenging pregnancy with triplets, and waded in and out of everyday life with one another. I have never felt so much gratefulness for a friend before than the morning after a particularly stressful day when sweet Marisa unexpectedly showed up at my door with a hot mug of white chocolate mocha, just to tell me she was thinking about me. How I love my friends. We are a group of women happily forced together by our individual acts of desperation to find community during our season in one of the most potentially isolating jobs on the market.

In fact, God has given me a double blessing in this mommy group. A few months ago, after I realized my life was getting easier to handle, I felt God's prompting to start a Bible study group for moms. I knew I could fill the group with ladies from our large church where there's always a demand for group leaders, but I wanted to offer it as an opportunity to other moms in my play group first. When I posted the opportunity, I was nervous that no one would respond and I would feel like a dork (again!). To my delight, I received a very positive response and now nine women meet in my home on a weekly basis to grow together as followers of Christ. So now we're walking side by side in sisterhood and faith as well as motherhood and friendship. What an amazing blessing!

More important than any other improvement though, is that I am at peace with myself again. Last year was a year of new things: new friendships, a new hometown, a new baby. It was tough trying to make myself at home in so many new situations. But now that my support system is in place and my household is once again at peace, I feel the stability of contentment accompanying me through each day. Those baby blues are finally a thing of the past! How can I look back on my journey and not thank God?! He never did promise that life would always be easy, but He did promise to always be with me. He has brought me this far. He is good.

A PROMISE

"Who am I, O Sovereign Lord, and what is my family that You have brought me this far?" (2 Samuel 7:18).

A PRAYER

Lord, remembering the journey I've completed and the way things were often so hard for me to handle, I am moved to sing praises to You for the blessings you have rained down on me! You have walked by my side, challenging me to grow and refining my character. You have blessed me with love, friendship, family, and peace. Thank You for Your good gifts!

Hindsight

A PERSPECTIVE

Ah, hindsight! If only I had the same wisdom at the beginning of a journey that I discover at the end! Nearly every page of this book is filled with my goofy mistakes. If I knew then what I know now, I would have chosen to:

Recognize my need!

I knew at the time that it was a challenging season for me. Peaceful was not the word I would have ever used to describe it. Yet, it wasn't until it was over that I finally recognized how stressful it had been and how much I had been in need. It was easy at the time to shrug it off and say, "Yeah, this is a crazy life, but I'm okay." But I wish I had the sense to say to myself, "Look, on a daily basis my love-tank is empty, my stress-levels are soaring, my peace-meter is crashing, and my engine is running on fumes. I need *something*!" Then maybe I could have had the sense to apply the rest of these insights!

Take time for myself!

For most moms on their second child, this is already a learned strategy. With one baby, I knew that I would be a fool not to use his rest time as my rest time. And I did this initially with two babies too. I have no problem sleeping when I need sleep. Everything else can wait.

But as the newborn got older, and everyone was sleeping a little better, something changed. I felt more rested and what I needed for myself wasn't really a nap anymore (most days). What I needed at mid-day naptime was more like a bubble bath, curling up with a good book, or a cup of hot tea. What I needed was a break. I needed to rest and rejuvenate my spirit to get prepared for the second half of each marathon day. But, I never fathomed taking time in the middle of the day just to nourish my spirit and recharge my batteries.

If I could go back to that time I would say, "Stop your busyness and take a hot bath!" The chores and projects, as well-intentioned as they might be, can wait. When I don't take some time to meet my own needs, everyone suffers.

Seek God's healing!

In an effort to heal myself, or pull myself out of the problem, my solution was to try harder, to press on, to do more, to get over it. Upon awakening like a groggy child into my new life as a mother of two, I bypassed the healing and rest offered by my heavenly Father. Rather than letting Him hold me until I was ready for action, like I do for Isaac when he wakes up grumpy, I instead dropped immediately to my feet yelling, "Now go, go, go!"

I had a million and one things to accomplish each day, and I treated my relationship with God as one of the numerous tasks on my list. I would sit down at the kids' nap-time, rush through my devotional reading, and mutter a hurried prayer before blasting past God on my way to my next task. He was just settling in to be with me as I raced away to *do* more. I bypassed His healing every time. No wonder I was so tired.

It reminds me of my oatmeal chocolate chip cookie fiasco. One day in college, I decided to cut back on the oatmeal in my favorite recipe, thinking it would be better without so many bland oats. With each consecutive batch, I cut out more and more of the oatmeal. And each batch was crunchier and less tasty than the one before. It continued until I brought my cookies to work one day and they were barely edible. You could hear people struggling to crunch into cookies from across the room. It was embarrassing. I had been making these cookies forever. Why was I having so much trouble getting it right? Instead of getting better and better, they were getting worse and worse! It finally dawned on me that it was the ingredient that I was *leaving out* that was causing the trouble.

It was just like cutting down my quality time with God in an overcrowded day. There were dozens of ingredients to my day. It was so over-packed with to-dos that I didn't see the harm in cutting down just one. So my time with God got cut shorter and shorter. Sure, I still sprinkled some in every day, but it was no longer a key ingredient. And then I began to wonder why the recipe was no longer working!

Instead of my extended to-do list, the only thing I should have been doing last year was to come before God and allow Him to heal me. I should have chucked the devotional and my agenda out the door and spent time resting (and weeping if necessary) in God's grace and love. I should have lain at His feet for every spare minute that I had, taking in as much of His strength and peace as I could. Imagine how different that year would have been if I would have done that. Instead of running on empty, I would have been filled each day with healing that only God can give. And He wants to give it! He even invites us: "Come with me by yourselves to a quiet place and get some rest" (Mark 6:31 NIV).

Stop comparing and accept the season!

Before I had Abby, I was witness to several other moms adjusting to their second babies. They took some weeks or months to adjust and then rejoined the rest of functioning society with apparent grace. I expected my own adjustment to be the same: a few months out of the loop and then back to normalcy. Initially I was okay with accepting my down time. And then one arbitrary day I decided it was time to be over it. I began to push too hard, too soon, to make myself achieve those to-do list items that I felt had been put off for too long. After all, if those other mothers could do it, surely I could too?

I needed to realize that every mother's story is unique just as every child is unique. Here's what I would say to myself if I could go back: "Hey Megan! So it looks like she's got the "mother-of-two" thing down and her baby's only three weeks old while you're still struggling to survive and your baby is a few months away from her first birthday? So what? You're not her. Stop trying to be! Accept yourself and your circumstances as unique and deal with the situation you've got! And remember, Girl, it's just a season (long though it may be). Be at peace with the season you're in, knowing in time it will get better."

Ask for help!

Even for me, new to the neighborhood, there were plenty of people who would have been willing to help if I had only asked. I received several casual offers to help, and most of the time I felt these offers were genuine. "Call if you need anything!" But, because no one yet knew me intimately, they did not feel comfortable forcing their help on me and I didn't feel comfortable asking. I should have asked!

Sometimes I tend to hibernate in my own little kingdom, separated from others by walls and fences. I like the isolation because I don't have to see the messes my neighbors get themselves into so I am not compelled to help clean them up. The problem with this system is that no one is there to help me with my messes either! I do believe it takes a village to raise a child and yet I can sometimes find myself village-less, isolated in a crowded world. Sure, I can get through motherhood on my own. I'm a strong woman. I was raised to be independent. I can survive! But wouldn't it be better for me to ask for help and *thrive*?

What if I had asked a friend to have my older child over to play for an hour every once in a while? What if another friend could take the baby every now and then? What if I had really followed up when the neighbor offered to bring us a meal? Every little bit helps, and people are generally happy to do it, but they often have to be asked! In my experience, the people I'm closest to are those who freely ask for help from me and give help to me. I have found that this exchange moves someone from an outsider to an insider in my life. It builds bridges.

Lower my expectations!

On one frosty morning I set out on a walk with my kids bundled up in hats, jackets, and blankets and with the windbreaker-top clipped down on the jogging stroller. My kids were plenty snug, even though I was fully exposed to the elements. Soon, I crossed paths with my retired neighbor who was just returning home from his walk around the lake. He informed me that the winds there were quite strong. I commented on how my ears always get so sore when I'm walking in that blasting cold wind. Right then and there, my sweet neighbor took off his hat (one that had grandpa-like earflaps) and offered it to me. I laughed good naturedly at what I assumed to be a joke, but he told me he was serious, I could use his hat if I wanted too. I took it from his hand with a reluctant smile.

The rim was dirty and the interior was scattered with some of his white hairs. It wasn't exactly what I had in mind for my own ideal creature comforts. I could easily have tossed the cap into my stroller basket. Instead, I pulled that warm cap over my ears and enjoyed a blustery walk around the lake without suffering the usual ear-trauma.

Sometimes when I lower my expectations, it allows me to accept the blessings that others offer. Imagine how sad it would have been if my neighbor had offered me the hat off his head and I had been too stuck up to accept it. What warmth and friendship I would have missed! Thank you, neighbor!

This philosophy could have applied equally to a meal from a friend that was slightly under par or a gift that was not exactly on top of my "most wanted" list. It's good for me to remember that everyone around me, just like me, is simply doing the best they can. (And I might as well apologize to any of the new moms who lowered their expectations and suffered graciously through one of my home-cooked meals. Cooking is not my forte!)

Shelve my good intentions (for a time)!

Every human being has room for improvement. One of my nagging weaknesses is unhealthy cooking. For a long time, I felt a huge burden of guilt every time I pulled out a box of mac & cheese. "I need to do better," I would think to myself as I cooked up some hotdogs for the third time that month.

And I made some efforts at improvement. I tried new recipes and introduced new vegetables into our diet. But my timing was off. My efforts fizzled as I tried to make improvements when my batteries were on empty and the kids made it nearly impossible to cook anything at all. In truth, I really did not have the time or patience to prepare anything more elaborate than a grilled cheese sandwich. Whatever the good intention, I needed to give myself permission to say, "I know that idea is the best way to go, but I really can't handle adding it to my plate right now. I'll shelve it for a while and come back to it later when I'm more capable of taking on a new skill."

Be selfish (for a season)!

While I was still in need of help and healing myself, I was faced with many opportunities to help others who were equally in need. Most of the time I rose to the occasion because I knew it was socially the right thing to do and I earnestly wanted to help others. But at what cost? Is it time well spent to take an evening to prepare for someone else a meal that's far more complex than what I normally feed my own family? What if, while I'm fixing that ambitious meal, my own children sit crying at my feet, wanting my attention? What if my own, gentle husband gets frustrated that I'm using my precious resources (time, energy, love…) to help another family while my family suffers the consequences? Is that really the "right" thing to do?

Looking back, I think perhaps not. We just weren't ready for that kind of thing and it was wrong of me to try to force it too soon. I'm not condoning a lifetime of selfish behavior. But I should have realized that I couldn't do it all and I needed to put my own family first. I'd like to go back and say to myself, "Megan, when it's all said and done, and life begins to be easier again; when your kids play happily together, allowing you to get some of your chores done on a regular basis; when your mind bursts with passion and creativity, your body feels energized, and your spirit feels ready to pursue your dreams; when the overall motif of your family time is peace: *then*, it's finally the time to turn your focus away from your family and help others."

Count My Blessings!

It's just as simple as that. I needed to (and indeed did) continually remind myself of all of my blessings. My beautiful children, my loving husband, my faith in God, my family nearby, my new friends, my home: all were blessings that carried me through.

Remember!

Now that I'm really ready, I can use my memory of how hard this job can be as motivation to help others in the same situation. So here are my on-going instructions to myself right now: "Megan, remember how gloomy some of those long afternoons were? Invite a new mother over for an afternoon playdate or to fix dinner together. Megan, remember how much you needed entertainment for your older child while you cared for your newborn? Offer to pick up a friend's oldest and take him to the playground with you and your kids. Megan, remember how hard it was to fix a decent meal while your little ones clamored for your attention? Help provide meals for your friends who have young ones. Megan, remember how much you did not want to have to ask for help? Don't wait for a friend to ask you! Go over to her house and tell her, 'Put some pants on that child...I'm taking him out for a playdate!'"

If I had truly grasped all these concepts before I had my second child, there would have been a lot less drama and this book probably would never have been written. Lovely thought. On the other hand, I don't really regret the challenges, seeing as how they prompted growth. My hope is that I will use this list as a reminder during my next challenging season. The next time I find myself in a taxing situation, I plan to: recognize my need, take time for myself, seek God's healing, stop comparing and patiently accept the season, ask for help, lower my expectations, shelve good intentions, be selfish for a while, count my blessings, and remember what it's like so that I can help others later! Most importantly, I will continue to ask God for wisdom. Just because I've learned a few things does not mean that I'm even close to the woman God wants me to be.

A PROMISE

"If any of you lacks wisdom, let him ask of God, who gives liberally and without reproach, and it will be given to him" (James 1:5).

A PRAYER

Lord, I am so thankful for the opportunity to reflect and grow through my challenges. I love and adore You for not only walking beside me but also for teaching me Your wisdom along the way. I ask You to help me use the lessons I have learned to be more prepared to face trials in the future (because they will come!). And I pray that You will help me to never stop learning and growing.

References

Barry, Dave (1984). <u>All the Dave Barry You Could Every Want</u>: <u>Babies and other Hazards of Sex</u>. USA: Rodale Inc.

Kingsolver, Barbara (1998). <u>The Poisonwood Bible</u>. New York: HarperTorch.

Numeroff, Laura Joffe (2002) <u>If You Give a Mouse a Cookie</u>. Naples, FL: Frederick Thomas, Inc.

<u>The Holy Bible, New International Version</u>. (1984). Grand Rapids, MI: Zondervan.

<u>The Holy Bible, New King James Version</u>. (1982). Thomas Nelson, Inc.

And so it goes…

Made in the USA
Lexington, KY
11 October 2012